Praise

'*Automatic Recruitment Agency* is a game-changer for the recruitment industry. Through his insightful exploration of the intersection between automation and recruitment, James Blackwell provides a roadmap for recruiters to modernise their processes, optimise their workflows, and drive better outcomes and higher profits. This book is a must-read for anyone seeking to stay ahead of the curve in the rapidly evolving world of recruitment.'
— **Benjamin Mena**, managing partner, Select Source Solutions, and host of *The Elite Recruiter Podcast*

'By reading this book, you will learn how automation and recruitment are like two sides of the same coin, working seamlessly together to revolutionise the hiring process. By harnessing the power of automation, recruiters can streamline their workflow, increase efficiency and ultimately make better hiring decisions.'
— **Hishem Azzouz**, founder, Recruitment Mentors, and host of *The Recruitment Mentors Podcast*

'James Blackwell has an X factor that is unique and powerful. Not only does he walk his talk when it comes to building multimillion-dollar businesses, but he possesses the rare quality of being able to teach others how to do the same in a way that cuts through the fluff. Read this book before your competition does and you'll see results faster than most entrepreneurs ever will.'

— **Peter Sage**, author of the number one bestseller *The Inside Track*.

AUTOMATIC RECRUITMENT AGENCY

Automatic Recruitment Agency

Scale to seven figures while **working less**

James Blackwell

R^e think

Contents

Foreword   **1**

Introduction   **3**

    Who this book is for   4

    The agency employee   6

    The sole agency owner   8

    Business skills and beyond   9

    The solution   11

    Getting started   13

1 Systematise To Automate   **15**

    Generating and converting clients   17

    Sourcing candidates   17

Systemisation 18

Automation 21

The delivery machine 24

Checklist 25

2 **Winning More Clients: A Proven Strategy** 27

Mapping the market 29

Client outreach 33

Coming back for more 44

Checklist 45

3 **Candidate Delivery System** 47

Candidate nurture 49

Candidate outreach through virtual assistance 58

Video outreach 62

Checklist 64

4 **Cash Flow** 67

Know your numbers 69

Speed up your cash flow 71

Trim the fat 73

Reinvesting in the business 74

From $100k to $1 million   76

Checklist   77

5   The CEO Plan   81

You're on your own   82

Delegating   89

Checklist   94

6   Hiring   95

How many?   98

Your virtual team   102

Who to hire   104

Checklist   107

7   Seven-figure Mindset   109

Find your mentors   111

Weekly group calls   116

Upgrading your peer group   119

Learning and development   122

Checklist   123

8   Investing In Yourself   125

Meditation   128

Daily routines   130

Wealth and happiness   134

Love   136

Checklist   137

Conclusion   **139**

The Author   **143**

Foreword

I am honoured to write the foreword for this remarkable book by James Blackwell. Put aside the millions of dollars, the Rolls Royce and fleet of supercars, the penthouse or the vast amounts of money he's spent to give back to his family – the key thing James has accumulated over the years is good will.

I've seen James at his lowest lows and his highest highs, and he has remained stoic through it all. He is one of the few men I genuinely admire. He's always had my back and been the brother I never had.

Not only is he one of the most kind-hearted people I've ever had the pleasure of meeting, but James can help you achieve your business goals. I've seen the way he operates, and I'm here to tell you first hand that you're learning from someone who has not only done it but done it in the right way – not by breaking backs, but by carrying the weight on his own shoulders, being an inspiring leader, a loyal friend and someone who never stops pushing.

In this insightful book, James explores the dynamic fusion of automation and recruitment. After reading, you will have a clear roadmap for modernising processes, optimising workflows, and driving exceptional outcomes and profits. It's a must-read for anyone in the recruitment field.

Iman Gadzhi, founder, IAG Media

Introduction

What was I thinking? In 2015, I had a stable job working for a well-known recruitment agency and earning a comfortable salary. I had just bought my first house, so I had a mortgage, overheads and bills to pay. Then I went and left the job, took out a personal loan of £10k and borrowed a further £10k on credit cards. It was a scary moment, I can tell you, but it was a leap of faith I was determined to take because I knew I could make a lot more money working for myself than for someone else.

I'd already owned a business once before – a coffee shop when I was twenty-one – and it had failed (of which more later), but I'd learned a lot from that experience. I'd also put my years working at the agency to good use and focused on personal development: I read business books after work and got up by 6am to listen to podcasts or watch YouTube videos to build my knowledge and confidence. You could say that my leap of faith was more of a calculated risk.

Why didn't I get a business loan? Well, a bank won't give you a business loan unless you have a proven track record, which I didn't at that time. I was offered investments by two separate entrepreneurs, one of them a prominent figure on *Dragons' Den*. I went to see him a couple of times, and he offered me a quarter of a million pounds to invest in the business in return for a large equity stake. I almost accepted his proposal, but luckily, I decided not to. I knew that I would just be exchanging one sort of control for another, when what I wanted was the freedom to do things my way.

There I was, out on my own, with the money I needed to launch my business and enough in the bank to cover three or four months of mortgage payments and bills. I knew that I would be needing some income soon, and that's when the real challenge began.

Who this book is for

If you're feeling frustrated with your current agency job and want to take control of your earning potential, this book is for you. I'll show you step by step how to start and grow a successful recruitment business. I'll share with you my personal story and the lessons I have learned along the way so you can avoid common pitfalls and achieve the financial freedom and flexibility you desire.

Starting your own recruitment business may seem like the ultimate dream – the chance to gain financial freedom for yourself and your family and to control your work schedule. The reality often turns out to be different. Many entrepreneurs find themselves swamped with responsibilities, struggling to make progress and seeing barely any financial reward as profits need to be reinvested back into the business.

The reason many go wrong is that they are trying to replicate a business model that they have worked for in the past. I knew I wanted to do things differently. It's my firm belief that we only get one life, and while making money is important, it shouldn't come at the cost of being tied to a business that drains you because if you don't turn up to work the business fails. A new era agency should not require you to be physically present every day to keep it running.

I understand the frustration of feeling limited in your earning potential and career growth in a traditional agency. As an agency employee, I knew there had to be a better way to earn money than spending over ten hours a day cold-calling while sitting at a desk in a suit, so I took the risk and started my own business – Ronald James.

On average, recruiters take home 20–30% of the revenue they generate for a business. This means an average recruiter who generates £150k–£200k a year for a company will keep £50k–£80k. After taxes, the take-home pay is closer to £35k–£40k, with a fifty-hour-plus working week.

Entrepreneurial recruiters can retain nearly 100% of their earnings by starting their own business, but where do you begin? How do you win clients and find candidates when starting from scratch?

That's where this book comes in.

The agency employee

Changing yourself from an employee to a business owner starts with changing your mindset and your daily habits, while also following a proven formula for business success. I was clear that I needed to become James Blackwell 2.0 to create the life that I aspired to, but without a guide or a mentor it's hard to make that transition.

The statistics bear this out: only 78.5% of businesses survive the first year and within five years half of new businesses have folded. What's more, 96% of businesses fail to reach a turnover of US$1m – 96%![1]

With only themselves to take care of, most solopreneur recruiters have low costs. They can take advantage of a beneficial tax position, and there is little other outlay: a LinkedIn licence, perhaps, and some other tools that I feature in my programme and will describe later in the book. This means that straight away you are looking at profit margins of around 75% and the possibility of reaching £100k, maybe more, in your first year.

How do you go about it? How do you win those all-important first clients and find those first candidates? If you're thinking about making this move, I can offer you a detailed road map, showing you step by step how to start building your business from first principles and establishing the pillars on which to grow your recruitment agency to six figures within the first year.

To follow your dream of setting up for yourself, you've got to be prepared to change, and to invest in yourself. In this book, I will show you the ropes for how to go it alone, but what has got you where you are today will not get you where you want to be tomorrow. You will

---

1   N Harnish, *Scaling Up: How a few companies make it… and the rest don't* (Gazelles, Inc., 2014)

have to consider who you need to become to achieve what you want to in life.

I have seen plenty of recruiters who have taken the plunge and found it a shock to the system. Suddenly they think, 'Help – where do I start? Back in my job I had a lot of support, a recognisable brand, a company name, all the back-office services, established clients and candidates, and now all that's gone, and this is ground zero.'

The sole agency owner

Too many solopreneur recruitment agency owners that I have come across are taking responsibility for every single task in their business: they are sourcing candidates; looking for leads for new clients; trying to convert those leads into paying clients; arranging interviews for candidates; managing their own diaries, email, websites and social media; creating their own branding; organising their marketing; and taking care of all the finance, operations and systems – and they're doing all this manually.

On any given day they are wearing a number of hats and jumping from one task to another in an unproductive way. They are on a hamster wheel, trying to run faster and faster but not getting anywhere because they're not building proper assets or establishing systems in their business that enable them to delegate or automate.

If this description fits you, chances are that you are working for your business rather than getting your business to work for you. It's time to modernise by systemising your business and leveraging technology so you don't have to do everything manually.

A lot of solopreneurs do well enough: they make a few placements and that might bring in, say, around £100k a year, but they can never go beyond that sort of figure because to do so they would need effective operations and perhaps a team. As Michael Gerber asserts in his book *The E-Myth Revisited*, they have to become a true business owner rather than just a business operator.[2]

Over the past three years, I've helped around 400 agency owners to build systems and assets in their businesses and become true CEOs. These entrepreneurs from all over the world have succeeded in starting, growing and scaling their agencies to six or seven figures.

Business skills and beyond

Anyone who has been working as a recruiter will have a well-developed set of recruitment skills, but – in

---

2   M E Gerber, *The E-Myth Revisited: Why most small businesses don't work and what to do about it* (Harper Business, 2001)

addition to a change of mindset – you also need some specific business skills. I would characterise the essential skills as follows:

- Systemising – identifying and automating repeatable processes to save yourself repetitive tasks

- Inbound marketing – knowing how to attract the right clients and candidates into your business

- Branding – understanding how to create an engaging image for your business

- Finance – balancing cash flow and reinvestment effectively

I would go so far as to say that at least 90% of top-billing recruiters who work for other people have tried and failed to get to six or seven figures in the agencies that they started. They ended up going back to work in an existing company simply because they didn't have the business skills they needed. They might have been good at being a salesperson on behalf of an agency, but once they had to wear twenty-five different hats a day they became overwhelmed and realised they didn't have the skill set they needed.

On top of this they may have been trying to recreate a traditional model – the one I call the 'Wolf of Wall Street' model – that 80% of agencies still operate on: lots of staff in an office, suited and booted, hitting the phones, with a sales director cracking the whip and challenging KPIs to meet. I know business owners in the industry who run such companies successfully, but most people don't want that level of stress and overwork with limited time off. Those that are prepared to put up with it are usually hoping to sell their business eventually, but it's a fact that 80% of businesses never sell.[3]

You'll also have to impose your own discipline. With no one above you to keep you on track, you are at risk if your motivation wavers. That's why a key part of my programme is accountability. It's a bit like having a personal trainer at the gym. You don't have one to show you how to lift weights; you have one to make you get out of bed in the morning, because you've paid for them to keep you up to the mark. The mutual accountability of a like-minded group is what keeps all its members on track.

The solution

Why not create a business that you love to work in? The ideal situation is to be either a solopreneur or to have a small team of up to twelve people, which is what I do. This allows you to ensure a profit, and

---

3   M Seiler Tucker, 'Why 8 out of 10 businesses don't sell', www. seilertucker.com/why-8-out-of-10-businesses-dont-sell (Seiler Tucker, 2 September 2020), accessed 23 February 2023

the business is practically self-managing. I can take multiple holidays a year because the business is built on solid foundations with the right systems and processes in place. Rather than overreaching and trying to scale aggressively and hire lots of people, I have created a boutique agency which is a hybrid between a lifestyle business and a medium-sized business.

Many lifestyle business owners in the recruitment field would have two or three virtual assistants (VAs), and through that approach they have scaled their businesses to up to £500k a year. They work four or sometimes only three days a week and get to spend more time with their families and on their leisure interests. When you move from a lifestyle agency to a boutique agency, you make a further leap from a six-figure business to a seven-figure one.

It's important to figure out which option is ideal for you and identify your true goal accurately. Many people who join my Agency Blueprint programme say they want to reach the magic million-dollar-a-year revenue mark, but what truly matters is the profit. The income you will need to fund your desired lifestyle, such as a nice house and car, leisure activities and holidays, a pension plan, etc, should be your main goal rather than an ever-expanding bottom line.

Getting started

Over the next eight chapters, I will guide you through the steps necessary to become a successful agency owner. Whether you're just starting out or are already running your own agency, this book will provide valuable information and practical guidance.

I recommend reading the book cover to cover, then keeping it on hand for reference later. Each chapter includes checklists to help you stay on track and there are links to useful resources on my website.

It's important to note that there are certain topics that I will not be covering, such as compliance, legislation and insurance. The requirements associated with these can vary greatly from country to country and it would be impossible to cover them all adequately in this book. Agency owners should nevertheless ensure they understand the importance of addressing these issues and taking responsibility for them.

Let's take the first step towards you becoming an agency owner rather than an agency operator by exploring how you can systemise your business.

ONE

Systematise To Automate

I had always dreamed of becoming a millionaire, taking six holidays a year and working no more than four days a week, but while employed at a traditional recruitment agency, I realised that their outdated approach would never get me there. I read Tim Ferriss's book, *The 4-Hour Work Week*,[4] and learned how he built systems that enabled him to outsource tasks and delegate to others. When I looked around at how we worked in the agency, it was clear there was a more efficient way of doing things than handling everything manually.

---

4   T Ferriss, *The 4-Hour Work Week* (Vermilion, 2011)

I started researching automation and VAs and saw their potential for transforming a business. Discovering this was frustrating because the company I was working for had its own set processes, so I couldn't implement any changes. The only way I was going to break free from cold-calling hundreds of people and working late every night was to start my own business and have autonomy to run things my way. I'd developed the concept of a systemised, automated recruitment agency, but could I put it into practice?

The first thing I needed was a modern, comprehensive model to replace the outdated one I had left. There are only so many hours in a day, a week or a month, and as a business owner you need to prioritise: to focus on the tasks that generate high income instead of, for example, following up on emails, which can be outsourced.

Of these tasks, the number one priority was getting clients, which makes sense because without clients, you don't have a business. I knew that there wasn't time to reach out to every prospect manually: cold-calling, leaving messages, sending emails, remembering to follow up – it's all time-consuming and doesn't allow you to grow your business effectively.

My new model is designed around four central pillars: generating clients and converting clients, creating a candidate sourcing system, systemisation, and automation. If you prefer to lead a small team, you may want to add a fifth: building a delivery machine.

Generating and converting clients

The most important first step in generating new clients is to define your niche market and map it. The aim is to engage with it in a way that is not too time-consuming, and this entails creating a client acquisition system to generate a steady stream of inbound leads. I have created a forty-slide pitch deck that has generated revenue worth over £4m over the past six years, and it has done this by enabling me to convert 80% to 90% of the people who responded to my pitch into signed clients.

Sourcing candidates

The traditional way of sourcing candidates is through connecting with them on LinkedIn, searching job boards or putting out an advertisement. What I needed was a consistent way of driving candidates into my agency, and that could be done via bolt-on automation. I've now created that with LinkedIn and email automation, and a candidate nurture machine.

Many candidates that agencies propose are in fact what we call 'passive talent', which means that they are not necessarily looking to move to another company – so timing is crucial. You might reach out to such a candidate on one day and they won't be interested. In two weeks' time, though, they might have fallen out with their employer and all of a sudden they're looking. You might not be reaching out to them at that precise moment, but another agency might be. What you need is a system that keeps you at the front of their minds by engaging with them every couple of weeks.

The candidate sourcing system that we have built is a blend of automation, email nurture, email engagement and candidate nurture serviced by a VA sourcing team. Our VAs work from the Philippines and reach out to candidates regularly. We also have a team offshore, based in South Africa, that does video outreach and voice note follow-ups, which works well.

This approach offers far more leverage, because the VAs' hourly rates are low compared with what an experienced recruiter or business owner would expect to receive for the higher-value tasks they perform, such as speaking to the well-qualified candidates booked into their diary by the candidate sourcing system.

Systemisation

I outlined earlier the framework that we have created, consisting of the client acquisition system, the client conversion system and the candidate attraction system. Each of these systems contains procedures that are in effect repeatable tasks, as does the administration of the business generally. I estimate that 60% to 70% of your recruitment business could be systematised: for example, your applicant tracking system (ATS) and customer relationship management system (CRM), and this could be extended to include regular procedures for posting adverts on your website and updating social media.

Some of the basic systems needed for the smooth running of your business are:

- Number/data systems to drive decision-making, accountability and results

- Planning systems to help you and your team take the simplest, most direct path

- Employee management and review systems to help get the best out of your team

- Financial systems to make sure cash is a source of fuel for your business and that you are not held back by the lack of it

- Onboarding and fulfilment systems that keep you out of the 'weeds' of the business while also giving your customers maximum satisfaction

- Marketing systems to drive consistent, repeatable growth

These alone will help you to be more strategic, have better team performance, and drive efficiency and consistency; and they will ultimately get you to the next level. Systems set you free and are the key to scaling fast while avoiding peaks and troughs.

The remaining 30% to 40% of activity has to rely on the human element, because, after all, recruitment is a people business. You are only as good as your team, in particular your highly skilled recruiters. The goal of all your systems and processes is for a well-qualified candidate to be speaking in person to one of these recruiters, and for that conversation – characterised by elements of selling, persuasion, influence and building a rapport – to lead to a perfect match between the individual and the post in question.

Building the automated systems is a task that VAs can help with. My mantra for such systems is to keep them simple, and therefore as accessible as possible to the people who need to use them. Although you may not necessarily find VAs who already have the technical skills to build such systems, it's perfectly possible for them to learn to do so on the job. It is well worth paying them to spend several hours on Google or YouTube mastering the use of the tools you want them to deploy.

Once you have systems up and running that are working well, leave them alone. If it's not broke, don't fix it. It's reasonable to consider, every six months or so, whether there's a way to make any of them simpler, quicker or more efficient, but change for the sake of change is best avoided. A lot of the tools and systems that we use are now five years old.

It is possible to over-systemise, though. If you focus on systemisation too much, it can be at the expense of income-generating tasks. Stopping a current system process to introduce another costs time and energy, so you need to be sure that it will be worth it.

Traditional model vs new era model

Traditional model	New era model
Searching for candidates on LinkedIn and job boards, and advertising	Driving candidates to the agency inbound
Walking clients through your offer on an individual basis	Using a consistent and proven method for client conversion
Undertaking much of the initial outreach yourself	Outsourcing initial outreach and administration to a VA
Using a 360 recruitment process	Installing automation
Being office-based	Fully systemising the agency
Cold calling	Relying less on the business owner

Automation

Technology makes the use of VAs possible, and they have revolutionised people's ways of working in many different industries. There are countless tasks that VAs can perform to support the work of a recruitment agency: building databases, running the CRM, managing LinkedIn, handling the email traffic and managing a range of projects.

As well as my regular VAs, with their comprehensive understanding of how my agency functions, I also use freelance VAs for a range of one-off tasks – for example, building my website or designing a PDF brochure. This type of support is only a click away. Some of the best sources for this freelance assistance are:

- Upwork.com

- Freelancer.com

- OnlineJobs.ph

The amount of software out there to support an online recruitment agency can be quite overwhelming, and there is an art to combining it all into a satisfactory process for your business. The tech tools stack that I have adopted and used for operating my agency and helping over 400 other agency owners includes:

- **Applicant tracking system:** Recruiterflow, Lever

- **LinkedIn automation:** Meet Alfred, Dripify.io

- **Email automation:** LinkedIn, Reply.io (for email outreach)

- **Managing VAs:** Hubstaff, TransferWise (for paying them)

- **Video outreach:** Loom, Vidyard

- **Operations:** Slack (to manage my business from my phone)

The main piece of advice I give is never to use an all-in-one system, because none of them can combine LinkedIn automation with email automation, video outreach and ATS and CRM systems. It works best to merge these separate and highly effective tools. If this technical challenge is not one that anyone in your team could take on, hire a systems integrator to undertake the task, which is something we advise on in the programme.

Perhaps the most important channel for my business is LinkedIn: we can message at scale through it, and this is a task that is easy to delegate to VAs. Our powerful ATS can handle multiple email touchpoints, follow-ups and tracking.

We've tested other technology tools and platforms where developers tend to hang out, such as GitHub specialist Facebook groups, but there is no substitute for having a full market map of all your clients, potential clients and candidates, with their email addresses, LinkedIn URLs and phone numbers. We do use Facebook, but that represents no more than 2% of our revenue. We also use Google, which means that anyone who visits our website is targeted with ads for our services.

The delivery machine

The final piece of the puzzle is developing a consistent approach for closing deals and placing candidates. As a solopreneur, you may eventually find that you want to step back from this aspect of the business. Some people love recruitment and thrive in the role, but for others it's just a means to an end. If this is the case for you, it's important to create a 'delivery machine' that can handle the process without your constant involvement.

To achieve this, you'll need to build an in-house team of high-performing delivery consultants. Keep in mind that simply offering a good salary won't be enough to attract top talent. Most recruiters are motivated by the opportunity to make money, so your agency should allow them to focus solely on closing deals. With the right model in place, these consultants should be closing an average of five deals per month. This will not only increase their commission and take-home pay, but also drive more revenue for your business.

It's important to remember that if you're constantly bogged down by the delivery process, you won't have the time or energy to focus on growing and scaling your business. Instead, you'll find yourself trapped in a highly paid employee role, chained to it by golden handcuffs.

Checklist

As you embark on the journey of transforming your recruitment agency from a traditional model to a modern, automated one, it's essential to have a clear plan in place to ensure a smooth transition. Whether you're just considering the move or have already taken the first steps, these are the key activities you should focus on to ensure success in transforming your recruitment agency into a modern, automated and profitable business:

- Create a comprehensive map of all the activities your agency undertakes. Understand the systems they are based on and identify areas where automation can streamline the process and save time.

- Prioritise client acquisition as your first focus. Without clients, you don't have a business. Develop a system for attracting clients that is efficient and effective, such as a targeted marketing strategy or a referral programme.

- Develop a signature sales system that is flexible enough to tailor to individual clients. This will enable you to effectively communicate the value of your services and convert leads into paying clients.

- Leverage the power of VAs to free up your time for high-income-generating tasks. VAs can handle various tasks such as building databases, managing your CRM and handling email traffic, allowing you to focus on growing your business.

- Invest time and resources into understanding the software that will enable you to automate your business. There are countless automation tools available, and finding the right ones for your agency can be overwhelming. Hire a systems integrator to help you navigate the options and implement them effectively.

- Decide whether you want to operate as a solopreneur or build a team. Plan accordingly and ensure that your systems and processes are in place to support your chosen approach. Building a team of A-player delivery consultants can help you scale and take your business to the next level.

- Stay organised, stay focused and watch your business grow.

TWO

Winning More Clients: A Proven Strategy

Starting my own recruitment agency was a daunting task, but I knew that a key component to success was winning more clients. I quickly realised that there was a lack of resources and frameworks to help me define my niche market and map out a strategy for acquiring clients. I knew that I didn't want to rely on cold-calling and that inbound marketing was the key to freeing me from that tedious task.

I began to research and read books on inbound marketing, automation and sales strategies. One book that stood out to me was Chet Holmes's *The Ultimate Sales Machine*.[5] Holmes's concept of a 'Dream

---

5   C Holmes, *The Ultimate Sales Machine* (Portfolio, 2019)

100' strategy – which suggests that it's more effective to target a small group of dream clients than a bigger but less suitable cohort – resonated with me, and I knew that I needed to implement it in my own business.

I began attending local business events and networking with entrepreneurs to build my agency's profile. I had been reading a book a week and listening to podcasts from different mentors, which gave me a wealth of knowledge about new strategies for automation and the theories of various business gurus. This allowed me to have meaningful conversations with business owners and demonstrate the value that my agency could bring to them.

One of my first potential clients was a tech company in the north-east of England. They had been working with a well-established recruitment agency for a long time and were not interested in changing partners, but they were impressed with my approach and the fact that I had reached out to them.

Not long after, the CEO of the company saw one of my email campaigns and forwarded it to their head of recruitment. This led to a meeting where I established a rapport with the head and discussed my wealth of experience in the field of IT recruitment. Although I didn't have a clearly defined signature sales system or a pitch deck at the time, I demonstrated my enthusiasm for delivering results. The company gave me a chance and I landed my first placement. From that one placement, we generated over US$1m in revenue over the next five years.

This experience taught me the importance of attending events, networking and building a relationship with potential clients. It also highlighted the need for a clear strategy for acquiring clients and the value of inbound marketing over traditional cold-calling methods.

As my agency grew, I continued to attend events and embrace networking opportunities, but I also implemented a more targeted approach to acquiring clients. I identified my ideal client and focused on reaching out to companies within that specific niche market. I also began to use automation tools to streamline the process and scale up my efforts.

In addition, I invested in creating a comprehensive and engaging pitch deck that clearly outlined the value that my agency could bring to potential clients. This helped me to convert more leads into paying clients and solidified my agency's reputation as a trusted and reliable partner in the industry.

Mapping the market

How do you define a niche and plan a market? Do you just look at what other people are doing, follow the model of those who seem to be doing well and hope for the best? I started by deciding I would base my approach on Salesforce, a US software company that successful recruitment companies had modelled themselves on, and that I would cover the whole of the UK. I soon realised that just because other recruitment companies had been successful in that niche didn't mean that I would be.

I needed to analyse the market to find out what type of revenue it could generate, where the gaps in the competition were and the availability of different types of candidates. I started doing this through the more formal routes, like joining Business Network International, and through immersing myself in networking in my locality, going to entrepreneur events, coffee clubs, etc to get a feel for the demand out there for IT staff.

Knowing there had to be a better way, I developed my framework on how to map out a niche. I knew it had to be candidate-driven, because I had to be sure that there were more vacancies that companies wanted to fill than there were candidates. Why would a company pay us to find them talent that they could easily locate themselves?

To illustrate how you drill down into a market, let's imagine you want to go into financial recruitment. You would start by picking three different job titles within the financial niche, such as financial controller, financial administrator and chief financial officer.

Then you would be specific as to location, for example, Birmingham.

I worked through the metrics to establish the ideal ratio between live jobs and candidates. I went on Google jobs, Indeed, LinkedIn jobs, typing in the different job titles in the market that I was interested in to see how many live, active agencies were operating in that area. I would then go back and repeat the process but this time to establish the number of candidates, and within that the number of candidates with specific job titles.

Building the data sets in Google Sheets enabled me to create the client market map, so I knew who was currently hiring and I could start to target them. I devised a metrics sheet on which I built the framework that enabled me to assess what a good market looked like. Now I was ready for a deep dive to discover my niche. Ideally, you want to have a niche within a niche, and you want to get to the point where you are the number one expert in your microniche, known and trusted in the market. Once you've done the basic mapping to identify your niche, you can fine-tune the details as you start to get into the market.

Building your Dream 100

There is a tested framework for mapping out your Dream 100. In my own case, I was looking at SMEs in my area of tech with anything between ten and

250 employees. I have always been keen to work with SMEs that are growing fast because I know that if my company gets into a partnership with them as they are starting out, they will always come to us for their hires as they expand. A lot of the clients that are still with us today, six or seven years on, began working with us in our first or second year.

This is not to say that we don't work with big corporations. We have worked with billion-dollar companies, such as a bank with hundreds of thousands of employees, but it took us a lot of time to get there and we did so five years after we had set up our business, by which time we had an impressive track record behind us. It's just a lot easier to reach out to an SME and get a response from them, and you can build a relationship and establish a rapport with the CEO, a founding director, a managing partner or another influential person in the company.

The great thing about the Dream 100 is that it's a fluid strategy. As things evolve in your niche and you start to learn more about the clients and the market, you may discover that some clients who you were initially pleased to have in your Dream 100 are not so attractive after all, perhaps because they are retrenching rather than hiring, or because they don't have a good reputation. They should drop off your list in favour of others.

Don't forget that your Dream 100 clients don't have to arrive all at once. This is a figure to aim for over time. You might start off targeting twenty to thirty of your Dream 100 and end up working with ten of them. As your business grows, you might find you have a Dream 200, of which you are now working with about 100. The aim is not to work with every single client within that group, but ideally with around a quarter of them.

Client outreach

Having done the mapping, I started to develop my client acquisition system. Now I could test in real life what worked well, and what didn't. Which emails, what LinkedIn automation, what type of video outreach gave the best results? The more meetings I had with prospects, and the more clients I closed, the more I refined what resonated with them. This enabled me to define my signature sales system and to design a sales pitch deck that I could use to walk the client through their problems and set out what our solution to them was going to be.

The signature sales system

Your signature sales system should be a process that is unique to your company, and one that creates an unfair advantage for it. It should be expressed through what I call the million-dollar pitch.

Your pitch deck should walk your prospect, your client, your avatar – whatever you like to call them – through your entire process from end to end, though it should be personalised each time to show that you recognise your prospect's problems and understand what they've tried to do so far to fix them. Then you can explore how your business is different and how you have created a unique process to help them achieve the result they are looking for. You can follow up with the client through an online proposal document that they can sign electronically.

To begin with, I would always front the pitches myself, as I was the face of the business. Once you get to revenue of £1.2m a year, you can probably hand this over to someone else. That's the beauty of the signature sales system: it's a repeatable process that you will get better and better at, but it is codified in a way that enables anyone to pick it up and follow it.

The biggest challenge for small-business owners can be whether they can duplicate themselves. They may be able to win big clients, but often the rest of their team can't. The signature sales system enables you to replace yourself and empower members of your team to win clients, increasing the number your agency can bring in.

Planning the outreach

An effective, reliable client outreach method is the result of careful planning and has specific stages, as illustrated by the flow chart below.

I focused on analysing the steps, identifying what worked and what didn't along the journey from getting a lead to converting it into a signed client, and on designing the right type of response template for every stage. These are eight steps I developed:

1. Source clients, build lists and automate emails.

2. Build and start email automation campaigns.

3. Export client leads.

4. Load Dripify campaigns to automate LinkedIn recruitment (connection only).

5. Use Zapier to integrate your apps – from Dripify to Google.

6. Nurture campaigns.

7. Run LinkedIn InMail campaigns.

Alongside this process, I spent money on various courses and programmes covering the best methodologies for recruitment agencies to get clients, choosing the elements that I thought would work well for me. The key steps I opted for were video outreach, email automation complemented by follow-up software, and creating a sales pipeline nurture funnel. You can download our client email campaign pack at www.theagencyblueprint.com/book.

Once you have comprehensive and up-to-date data sets, you can begin to nurture potential clients as appropriate with emails in different volumes and frequencies tailored to their requirements, and video outreach. If you have a marketing team in house, you can do a lot more in the way of social approaches to candidates that are not related to specific vacancies. This could include invitations to webinars, offers or competitions. We also do live tech events and invite our clients to be guest speakers. They are occasions for learning, but also for relaxing with drinks and pizza, and I usually bring my whole team to them. You couldn't wish for a better networking opportunity.

We follow up on the outcomes of such events through our niche event maximiser, and it's clear that they represent added value for both clients and candidates. At the same time, they position me and my team as the experts in the field.

Campaigns

The next stage is to create your different campaigns, targeting the individuals on your database appropriately. These campaigns should include:

- Email automation

- Email nurture aimed at generating warm leads

- LinkedIn automation

- Warm LinkedIn follow-up

- Video outreach

I had worked out the metrics and established how many people we would need to approach to get a certain number of clients. To begin with, if I did between three and five pitches a week, I'd close 60% to 70% of them. The more I pitched, the more defined the process became, and the better I got at delivering it, and eventually I was closing at least 80% of my pitches.

The people we approach can get back to us through any channel that is convenient for them. Those that we don't hear from are put on a list for us to follow up in ninety days' time. Just because they haven't responded to us on this occasion doesn't mean they won't work with us in the future. I can point to a large number of my present clients who, in the first two or three years of my business, told me that they didn't like my company and wanted to unsubscribe from my emails, and whose founders or hiring managers refused to see me.

What changed? In the third year of my business, they came to a free event that I organised on the theme of hiring managers. Finally, they saw the value that I had to offer, and I secured the meetings I'd been after for so long. By then, of course, I had some impressive case studies to show them and a compelling sales pitch deck – and they went wild.

Understanding what it was about the other agencies that so frustrated companies allowed me to carve out an unfair advantage, and to present our USP clearly. Soon we were delivering placements to more and more clients, and we reached a point where it was no longer feasible to go out and meet every one of them, but now I didn't need to do this anyway, because clients were finding their own way to me – thanks to inbound marketing. I could walk them through my pitch deck and ideally win them as retained clients, working exclusively with me.

Introducing an automated client email system

The first requirement for an effective client email system is good-quality data to populate it with. We usually outsource the compilation of the data, but we will refine it ourselves, ensuring that all the email addresses are verified. Then it's time to load them into an email system, such as Rely.io. You will need to keep refreshing the data every six months, but this is a one-off task you can outsource to a freelance researcher.

It wasn't all plain sailing, though, and sometimes I learned the hard way. I ran a big email campaign when I launched my business, based on automation and follow-ups, but I didn't hyper-personalise my outreach and I hadn't mapped the market accurately. I soon realised that a lot of the potential clients I was reaching out to were the wrong ones.

The messages were wrong, and the response sequence didn't work. I ended up with an inbox full of replies, many from people who weren't happy. You can imagine how annoyed they became with the automated follow-ups that I didn't know how to prevent. It was a big campaign, too – over 3,000 people – which of course generated a huge volume of replies, and I had no idea how to organise them. I couldn't even answer them in a timely fashion. We lost a lot of potential clients because our system just didn't have the backend to handle all those leads. You have to strike while the lead is hot.

I learned a lot from that experience, I can tell you – not least that you can't just fix one thing, you have to build the full process. In the end I created a sales pipeline to manage these leads through a well-defined workflow, and this is where having a VA was invaluable, because she helped me to organise my inbox and nurture replies. All was not lost.

The final point to note is something you're probably well aware of, but as it's important I'm going to set it down here anyway: all your email communications must be compliant with the General Data Protection Regulations (GDPR). As a business, it is legitimate for you to message another business, but you are not entitled to send messages to personal email addresses, so your lists should contain company email addresses only.

Just as important is having a good subject line, because you want people to open the email. If you're anything like me, you'll check your inbox every day, but 80% of the emails you won't even open. They'll be consigned to Trash, Spam or Promotions.

Next you need good body text, particularly the opening paragraph, because you want people to read the message. The examples below show you exactly how a good email is structured.

Effective email copy is crucial for acquiring new clients and generating revenue for your agency. In my experience, crafting compelling and persuasive emails has been a key factor in earning seven-figure sums annually for my agency. To structure an effective

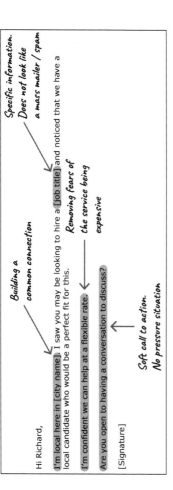

The problem, hook, solution email

Building a common connection

Specific information. Does not look like a mass mailer / spam

Hi Richard,

I'm local here in [city name] I saw you may be looking to hire a [job title] and noticed that we have a local candidate who would be a perfect fit for this.

Removing fears of the service being expensive

I'm confident we can help at a flexible rate.

Are you open to having a conversation to discuss?

Soft call to action. No pressure situation

[Signature]

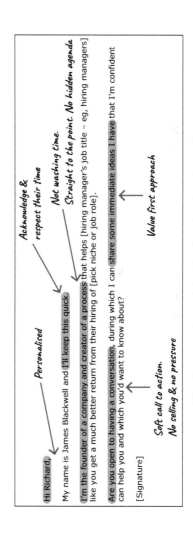

The three-sentence introduction, hook, ask email

Acknowledge & respect their time

Not washing time.

Straight to the point. No hidden agenda

Personalised

Hi Richard,

My name is James Blackwell and I'll keep this quick

I'm the founder of a company and creator of a process that helps [hiring manager's job title – eg, hiring managers] like you get a much better return from their hiring of [pick niche or job role].

Value first approach

Are you open to having a conversation, during which I can share some immediate ideas I have that I'm confident can help you and which you'd want to know about?

Soft call to action. No selling & no pressure

[Signature]

email, it is essential to have a set of templates that can be tailored to different clients, but the language is just as important as the structure. Using the right words and phrases can help to create positive emotions and generate interest in your offer.

For example, when targeting a specific new client, it can be effective to demonstrate that you understand their current situation and needs. This could be done by mentioning that you've noticed they are currently hiring and offering to provide them with a selection of relevant candidate profiles.

It's important to have a clear plan for the follow-up after an initial reply. For example, crafting an email that leads to a phone or Zoom call can be crucial for closing the deal. This is an important aspect of your sales system that needs to be defined and refined. Some examples of persuasive words and phrases that can be used in emails include: 'Exclusive', 'Limited time offer', 'Proven results', 'Customised solution', 'Free consultation'.

Remember, even if your email generates a reply, it doesn't necessarily mean that you've won the client. It's important to have a well-thought-out follow-up strategy to convert that initial reply into a successful deal.

Video outreach

Video outreach is a powerful tool that can significantly increase the impact of your emails. By attaching videos to your emails, you can create a more personal and engaging experience for your potential clients. There are two main types of videos that you can use – generic videos targeting a group of potential clients, or individual videos aimed at a specific hot lead.

When creating your videos, there are some basic rules to follow to ensure maximum effectiveness:

- Be yourself – viewers can always spot when people aren't being sincere.

- Smile – it creates a positive and welcoming energy.

- Make the video about the potential client, not about yourself.

- Flatter the potential client to make them feel special and valued.

- Offer value – for example, providing tips on where to look for candidates.

- Position yourself in front of a clean white background to avoid any distractions from your message.

To record your videos, you can use tools such as Loom or Vidyard. Once the video has been sent, potential clients can respond via email or LinkedIn, and the next step would ideally be a Zoom meeting.

Coming back for more

When it comes to building repeat business, it's important to keep your current clients engaged and satisfied with your services. To achieve this, you can add different features to your service, such as hosting events, creating cool video campaigns on LinkedIn, and featuring microsites on your website, such as a career site. You can invite clients to sponsorship events and add a personal touch to your professional service; for example, by taking clients to sporting events, sending small gifts at Christmas and reaching out to them regularly via WhatsApp groups.

It's important to remember that it takes a long time to successfully onboard a client, so it's crucial to retain them once they've been acquired. Occasionally, you may need to let a client go; for example, when a new manager has adopted new ways of working that are not compatible with yours, or when something has happened to make their brand not one you want to be associated with. By maintaining a good client acquisition system, you can ensure that you have a steady flow of new clients to replace any that you may lose.

Building repeat business is key to the success of your agency. By providing a reliable and fulfilling service, you can earn a reputation for excellence and attract new clients through word-of-mouth referrals. With a solid client acquisition system in place, you can turn on and off the flow of new clients as needed and maintain a balance between repeat and new business. This will allow you to build a self-managing agency that thrives on inbound client enquiries, with a steady stream of new clients asking to work with you because of your reputation as the best in the market.

Checklist

To ensure success in building a strong and sustainable agency, it's important to have a clear and concise checklist in place to follow when building and maintaining your client acquisition system:

- Clearly define your niche market and focus on SMEs that are growing fast. These businesses will be more likely to come back to you as they expand.

- Gather comprehensive data on possible job titles and update it regularly. This will be the basis for your email outreach and will ensure that you're reaching the right people.

- Create an email with an eye-catching subject line and compelling copy that highlights the value that your agency can bring to the potential client.

- Use generic or personalised video outreach to enhance the impact of your emails.

- Build and maintain relationships with clients, regularly reach out to them to offer added value, and make an effort to build personal relationships. This will help in retaining clients and getting repeat business.

- Continuously evaluate and improve your client acquisition system, taking into account any changes in the market, client needs and your own agency's performance.

THREE
Candidate Delivery System

When I first set up my own agency, I was using traditional methods to find candidates, such as LinkedIn, job boards and advertisements. It quickly became clear that these methods were time-consuming and not much different from what other agencies were doing. This led me to create a strategy based on automation and to explore how we could create more LinkedIn profiles to connect with our candidate markets and generate more conversations.

As with clients, we created a candidate map, collating details first in a Google Sheet and then in an ATS, which is essentially a CRM system for candidates. Once we had completed our candidate market map, we could start using data finder tools to 'scrape' emails and profiles of potential candidates within our niche area. This allowed us to reach out to them via email or LinkedIn.

It wasn't long before I realised, thanks to Tim Ferriss's book, that we could leverage low-cost virtual assistance to automate many of the routine tasks of locating, adding and reaching out to candidates. By outsourcing these tasks to VAs, we could focus on speaking to candidates who had expressed an interest in working with us.

Our first placement was for a small fee of US$2k for an IT support engineer, and our average fee is now around US$10k. I learned that being the cheapest doesn't mean you're the best and you can't base building a business on charging the lowest fees. We stopped working with that client immediately after this placement because they expected everything for nothing.

It's important to note that sourcing candidates proved to be much easier than building our Dream 100 list of clients. With a solid candidate delivery system in place we could then efficiently and effectively connect with potential candidates and place them with the right clients.

Candidate nurture

Your ultimate goal for an effective candidate delivery system should be to have in your database at any given moment a strong field of interested individuals who are experienced in your niche market.

Identifying candidates

The starting point for locating candidates is an accurate tagging system. You need to be aware of the range of possible job titles in your niche. There is greater variation in job titles than there is in client titles, so you might want to look at up to ten different possibilities. This means that it's also important to operate a tagging system that groups candidates together so that you don't miss those who are suitably qualified when you are doing a search. If, say, you are specialising in software engineers in a specific geographic location, you need to be aware of the range of variations on that title in use on LinkedIn, on job boards and on relevant blogs so that you can base your search on all of them. You also need to add tags reflecting technical skills – in the case of software engineers this could be, for example, specialising in PHP or JavaScript.

Once you have defined the range of terms, you can hand them to your VA to run the searches. Let's assume you are looking for software engineers in London.

You create the tag 'PHP software engineer – London' and all its possible variants. With this tag, it's easy to drill down and reach out to every software engineer with one technical skill in a particular location. This is the first step, and getting it right is vital. (For obvious reasons, we place a 'do not contact' tag on any candidates who are already working for one of our clients.)

The second step is to gather all the data you need. Google Sheets are ideal for this. The task of the VA, or perhaps a software tool, is to scrape LinkedIn and job boards for all the people with your range of job titles in a given location, placing all the data in the spreadsheet. Now you have a list of candidates for whom you (or ideally your VA) need to find email addresses and LinkedIn URL profiles.

Once you have these you can go back at a later stage to use a LinkedIn automation tool to connect with the candidate, sending them a message. Before you do this, though, you need to consider data protection regulations. Although the UK has left the EU, it still has its own version of the GDPR. This means you can only store email addresses if you have a legitimate business interest for doing so. To ensure that you are not infringing this (and some might argue that keeping data on individuals who have not contacted you could not qualify as a legitimate business interest), I would recommend using email tools such as Lusha and SignalHire.

If an email address is found by using either of these tools, you can argue that retaining it constitutes a legitimate business interest, because at some point candidates will have put their details on an open domain or out into the public realm. (If, when you reach out to them, they question where you got their details, you can point to authorised access to them – but of course you should offer to remove them from your database if they are not happy with being on it.)

We do sometimes get replies from candidates specifically about the GDPR issue, and in this case my advice is always to be proactive: a delivery consultant should contact that candidate and apologise. The more human the face you present the better: acknowledge that they must be sick of being inundated with spam, offer a personal apology, promise to remove them from the list and not contact them again – but explain that the reason you got in touch is that you are a specialist in this market, working with companies similar to the one they are in. As a compromise, you could undertake to alert them about any specific post they might be interested in in the future, and/or to contact them less frequently.

Rating the candidates

To enhance the available information about the candidates and make it easier to assess their suitability for a given role, we operate a candidate rating system that takes into account how many years' experience they have and what type of company they are currently working in – is it a reputable company within our niche, with a good track record of employing effective software engineers?

You need to have been in your niche for some time to develop an effective and responsive rating system. It becomes more refined and accurate as you get to know clients' needs and recognise the types of candidates who are likely to fulfil them. Clients vary tremendously in how demanding they are, and you will want to base a more detailed assessment of candidates on their requirements. I have found it useful to draw up a list of assessment criteria that broadly represent the most common client requirements in our particular niche. If you draw them up as concise bullet points or questions, these criteria will generate valuable metrics to help with your placement of candidates. Examples of these assessment questions could include:

- Has the candidate done the job before?
- Do they have the motivation to do the work?
- Have they used the necessary skills in their current role?
- How relevant is their experience to the role?
- Are they a good fit for the environment/culture – eg corporate vs startup?

- What trend does their performance show over time? Have they progressed in the last three to five years?

- What goals and ambitions do they have?

- Do they have untapped potential?

- Do they display leadership qualities?

- Do they display potential for retention? For example, have they stayed three to five years in a particular job?

We also rate the candidate's suitability for the role based on their requirements. Examples of these criteria could be:

- **Reasons for leaving:** Why did they leave their last role, or why are they thinking of leaving their current role? It's important to understand these reasons so that we can circle back to them and urge the candidate to consider them if they receive alternative offers – eg there may not be opportunities for progression. If they struggle to give a reason, ask, 'If you were the boss, what would you change/have changed?'

- **Main motivators:** The market is more competitive than ever, so you need to understand exactly what your candidate is looking for. Ideally they should provide three motivators ranked in order of importance. Focusing on these factors will enable you to sell a role by concentrating on the relevant areas.

- **The human aspect:** Be personal. How do the person's family feel about a potential career change? Do they have children? What sort of work–life balance are they looking to achieve? Look for interests and hobbies on the candidate's CV and try to find a mutual interest. It will help them to be more open.

- **Money:** What is the person's current salary? What benefits are important to them? What salary are they looking for? Don't focus on money, but make it clear that the person can trust you when it comes to negotiating on their behalf. Explain that the more you get for them, the better it is for you.

Reaching out

Now that you have got all the contact details, it's time to reach out to the candidates. They might not be actively looking for a new post when you contact them; they might not even reply to you, but in two weeks' time…

A lot can happen in two weeks. Your candidate may have fallen out with their boss, or the company may have decided to relocate and the candidate doesn't want to move with it – the possibilities are endless.

If you happen to reach out to them at that point, it will be perfect timing. This is why it's important to have a productive candidate nurture system in place, engaging regularly with the talent. It simply would not be possible to maintain this level of engagement as a traditional 360-degree recruiter who also has to be generating leads, winning clients, arranging interviews, etc.

If you put your candidates into a nurture system based on email automation, you can reach out to them every two weeks, six weeks, twenty-four months – whatever seems appropriate. To this you can add a routine for your VA to go into your ATS and create crafted messages for individual candidates, to search for anyone who hasn't been messaged in, say, the last thirty days and contact them through email and LinkedIn. There are four stages in the nurturing system:

1. **Sourcing candidates:** Source suitable candidates through the relevant team.

2. **Candidate approval:** Approved candidates move to the next stage.

3. **Email automation:** Approved candidates enter the ATS system and start to receive automated emails.

4. **Dripify campaigns:** LinkedIn campaigns run and the VA reaches out to all candidates via video outreach.

The first objective with candidate nurture isn't always to sell a position. If we get a reply, we will be able to open a conversation with them. As a team who live and breathe employment in their niche, we have a lot to offer them, including valuable career advice. We will be looking at a number of possible message sequences, but our opening line is usually something along the lines of: 'I appreciate that you might not be looking for a new post at the moment, but I thought I would reach out to you because we specialise in…' This is clearly an approach personalised to them, tailored to their niche, and you could go on to do one or more of several things:

- Pitch a role to them

- Offer some career advice

- Invite them to an event or a webinar

A message template for your VA to use when reaching out to candidates could be:

Subject: Connecting with a specialist in [niche]

Dear [Name],

I hope this email finds you well. I came across your profile on LinkedIn and was impressed with your experience and expertise in [niche]. I wanted to reach out and connect with you as we specialise in placing top talent in [niche] roles within growing companies.

I understand that you may not be actively searching for a new position at the moment, but I wanted to offer my assistance in any way I can, whether it's providing career advice, discussing current market trends or keeping you updated on any exciting opportunities that may arise.

If you're open to it, I would love to schedule a call with you to discuss your career goals and how we can help you achieve them. Additionally, I would like to invite you to our upcoming webinar on [topic], where we will be discussing [topic] and how it can benefit your career.

Let me know if this is something you would be interested in, and we can schedule a call at your convenience.

Best regards,

[Your Name]

As you can see, this email approach is a friendly and personalised way of reaching out to potential candidates. It focuses on building a relationship with them and offering value, rather than just trying to sell them a job. It also provides them with an opportunity to learn more about their industry and how they can improve their career through the webinar invite.

Candidate outreach through virtual assistance

In addition to making your agency more omnipresent in the market, VAs can greatly improve the efficiency of your candidate outreach efforts. They can handle tasks such as searching for potential candidates, reaching out to them via email or LinkedIn, scheduling interviews and tracking their progress throughout the hiring process. This frees up your time to focus on the more important tasks, such as evaluating candidates and closing deals.

When working with VAs, it's important to clearly communicate your expectations and provide them with detailed instructions on how to carry out their tasks. This can include creating a standard email template for them to use when reaching out to candidates, providing them with a list of specific job titles and keywords to search for, and setting clear guidelines on how to handle any objections or questions that may arise during the outreach process.

Another important aspect to consider when working with VAs is to ensure that they are well trained and equipped with the necessary tools and resources; for example, you could provide them with access to your ATS or CRM and any other software or tools they may need to effectively carry out their tasks.

CANDIDATE DELIVERY SYSTEM

Overall, using virtual assistance for candidate outreach can be an incredibly powerful tool for any agency looking to improve their efficiency and reach more potential candidates. By leveraging the expertise of a VA, you can free up your own time, gain more traction in the market and streamline your candidate outreach efforts.

CASE STUDY: Progress not perfection

Before joining The Agency Blueprint programme, Neil faced the challenge of trying to systemise his business. He had tried to implement some systems in the past, but they were vague and lacked structure, which hindered his ability to grow his business effectively.

After joining The Agency Blueprint programme, Neil quickly implemented the advised systems, and the effect was significant. The programme provided him with a proper structure and allowed him to streamline his business effectively. Neil also learned about perfectionist paralysis, which had hindered his progress in the past. He overcame this challenge by focusing on implementing the systems advised by the programme rather than striving for perfection.

After only six weeks of this approach, Neil achieved remarkable results. His deals and current pipeline have increased significantly, with a pipeline just short of 19k. If annualised, this is an uplift of 490k, which is an outstanding achievement. Neil attributes much of his success to the tools and structure provided by the Agency Blueprint programme.

Neil's success story is a testament to the effectiveness of a systematic approach. By implementing the programme's systems, Neil overcame his challenges, streamlined his business and achieved outstanding results. His experience is a valuable lesson for any recruitment agency looking to improve their productivity and grow their business.

The activity inventory

There are so many ways that VAs can contribute to your agency that it's useful to draw up a comprehensive list of routine tasks. This is something we cover in detail in The Agency Blueprint programme.

We walk through what you do on an hourly, daily and weekly basis, and as we identify each task, we can see exactly which ones can be outsourced or delegated to a VA. In my own agency, we have two types of VA: one is a general VA, who does more of the work that a personal assistant would do, and then there is a VA sourcer, who spends all their time on LinkedIn, the job boards or our ATS, reaching out to candidates, replying to them and selecting ones for us to follow up. In terms of metrics, this VA has a target of generating one placement per month. If they work full-time for our business, they are likely to be earning US$600–US$800 a month, yet the agency will receive US$8k for the placement. You can see that you get an excellent return on your investment (ROI) in a VA.

If you reverse-engineer this target, it represents just over one interview a week, with candidates sourced by the VA, who will have been given a target of picking five discovery calls a week for the delivery consultants to make. Of these, at least one should turn into a candidate whose CV you send to a client and for whom you receive a request for an interview in return.

I would caution that VAs should not speak directly to candidates. I know some companies have tried this, but it hasn't worked well. Part of recruitment is influencing or persuading a candidate over the phone, and a recruiter needs expertise to conduct a skilled conversation that deals with the candidate's life, their aspirations and their particular circumstances. VAs are not likely to be familiar with the culture in which you are operating, and it could damage your reputation if you attempt to use them on the sales side in this way.

The value of a VA doesn't lie only in the placements, though. Remember that they are there, reaching out all the time under your brand and creating your omnipresence in the market. The candidate they don't succeed in bringing in this month may become an inbound candidate next month, because they will remember your outreach. This ongoing marketing effort builds up the number of candidates in your ATS and on your LinkedIn profile.

CASE STUDY: The power of virtual assistants

Cheryl, a member of my elite mastermind programme, is a great example of how effective virtual assistance can be in growing an agency. She runs her agency from home and only works three days a week, yet she consistently achieves six figures in revenue. This is thanks to her virtual team, who handle the majority of her placements, allowing her to focus on growing the business and spending more time with her family.

In one month, Cheryl secured £42k in accepted deals, and onboarded a new VA from the Philippines as a sourcer, who was performing well. She also hired two new senior account managers to start the following January. She spent a lot of time on her client acquisition system and hired an expert in Zapier to implement automation that she wanted but didn't know was possible. This resulted in a successful December for her agency.

Cheryl's experience is a testament to the power of VAs in streamlining recruitment processes and freeing up time for business growth and personal pursuits.

Video outreach

There are two ways of going about video outreach, just as there are for client acquisition: generic and personalised.

Every time you get a new job in from a client, you should record a short Loom video – no more than three minutes – defining the sales pitch for the company in question. Your video should set out:

- Why a candidate should work for this particular company

- What the benefits are

- What the purpose of the job is

- What the career progression prospects are

It should also include a screen share of the company's website and information about their background. This is something that your VA can send out to the candidates on your ATS who have been tagged for such a role, alongside the actual job specification.

If they're interested, they'll open the email and watch the video, and if you have the right tracking set, you will be able to see who has done this. The ones who have watched the video are the hot prospects that you need to follow up personally.

Alternatively, rather than sending a generic message to, say, 150 candidates, you could opt to deploy the second strand of a video strategy: the hyper-personalised one-to-one video message. For this, you will pick out the ten to fifteen candidates who are most suitable for the job, and record a custom video for each of them, lasting not more than ninety seconds.

Having reviewed their LinkedIn profile, you might approach them with a message along these lines:

> Hi [Name],
>
> I can see that you've been working at X company for about four years now, and it looks as though you've progressed well – congratulations on that!
>
> The reason I'm reaching out to you is that I've got a unique opportunity at Y company that I'd like to discuss with you, and I think it would make sense for us to have a quick call. If you'd prefer, I can send you over the job spec for you to have a look at in your own time, and then you can come back to me with any questions.
>
> [Signature]

Checklist

With an effective candidate delivery system, you will have at your fingertips a good field of experienced individuals highly suited to placement with your clients. To build and maintain your access to this wealth of talent, you need to:

- Create accurate tags to enable you to identify candidates in your niche.

- Gather information on your candidates, including email addresses and LinkedIn URL profiles.

- Leverage virtual assistance both for creating your database and keeping in regular contact with candidates.

- Operate a consistent and responsive candidate rating system.

- Craft a personalised response to your hot prospects.

- Make full use of the potential of video outreach.

FOUR
Cash Flow

When I was twenty-one, in 2008, I was given the opportunity to run my own business. A family friend owned a coffee shop in Durham and was looking for an owner-operator to take over. I had been dealing cars from home and had saved up around £8k. I sold my car and combined the money with my savings to buy the stock that came with the business and take over the rental payments on the unit.

I employed four members of staff and was in the business every day, getting up at 6am to go to the cash and carry or driving to wholesalers to get stock, then filling up the shelves, among other jobs. The cafe was located in the heart of Durham and offered a variety of products, such as coffees, pastries, sandwiches, newspapers and confectionery. All sorts of people came in, including tourists and schoolkids. I worked seven days a week to keep it going.

The biggest challenge I faced was that I couldn't get any kind of loan, so I had to run the business off the cash flow I could generate. This meant I had to keep going to the cash and carry, and sometimes the shelves would be empty because I had to wait to make more money before I could refill them.

The problem was that I had absolutely no business experience. I could hustle, had sales skills and wasn't lacking in grit, but I didn't know how to go about the process of running a successful business. I didn't understand how important cash flow was and I didn't have a bookkeeper. I had to keep juggling my suppliers and delaying paying invoices until I had enough money. I had loads of invoices and receipts but nothing electronic, and I didn't have a clear idea of how much the business was taking in every month. I was too busy to focus on the cash flow.

Despite these challenges, I was awarded Young Entrepreneur of the Year for Durham in 2008. I was turning over £250k a year, but we weren't equipped to cope with the slow periods over the summer. I made a lot of effort to keep the cafe going, letting go of a couple of employees and working even more in the business myself. After two years of this, I felt I couldn't continue. I was sacrificing my personal life, going out with my friends and all the things that people in their early twenties normally do. I decided to close the business down and I handed back the keys.

With hindsight, this venture taught me some valuable lessons:

- You can't trade time for money, because it's not scalable – there are only so many hours in a day.

- It's hard to be profitable when certain sales items have profit margins lower than 30% and you have high overheads such as rental for a retail unit – as with a coffee shop.

- Last but not least, cash flow is king.

I realised that I was never going to grow and succeed without some personal development. How could I have thought that I could compete with the likes of Starbucks and Costa over the road, with the billions that they have behind them? I needed to find a business model that would generate healthy cash flow.

Know your numbers

Cash flow is a crucial aspect of any business and it's essential to understand the movement of money coming in and going out. In simple terms, a healthy cash flow means having enough funds at any given moment to cover your expenses and overheads. Without cash flow, your business is insolvent. You always need more money coming in than going out, and it's crucial to have money in the bank and not just rely on invoices that may or may not be paid in the future. Negative cash flow is dangerous, so it's vital to keep on top of it.

In my business, I have a report that keeps track of the amounts coming in and going out, and I check it regularly. It's OK if it's negative for a week due to bills, but it's crucial to know it will be turning positive soon.

One of the benefits of a recruitment agency is that you don't have to buy stock or inventory and you have fewer overheads, such as electricity bills or wage costs. It allows for higher profit margins, but it's still essential to have a clear and detailed picture of what's happening on a weekly basis. This includes being aware of every single expense going out and every placement fee or payment for other invoices coming in. I check my business bank account every day.

One number that is important for me is the average cost of my overheads for the last three months. This is something I ask my accountant to calculate, and then I can compare it with the fees that I know will be coming in. If I know that my average overheads are US$50k for a month, including salaries, commissions and all other costs, and there is US$120k to US$150k coming in over a month in terms of fees due, I can be sure we're in a good position. Ideally, your costs should represent less than 40% of your revenue. This means that your net profit margins should be at least 60%.

Speed up your cash flow

Getting cash in as soon as possible is crucial for any small business, but it's not always easy to get clients to pay promptly. Two strategies that have worked well for me are offering discounts and automated invoicing.

Discounts

When you send out invoices to new clients, offer a 5% discount if they pay within seven days. For example, if a £10k fee was due, the client saves £500. This has been a game changer for my business, as the revenue came in a lot faster than it would have otherwise.

Automated invoicing sequence

We use Xero for all our invoicing – a system that sends out reminders to clients when their invoices are seven, fourteen, twenty-one days and a month overdue. Any that have not been paid after a month go on a list compiled by my PA. Then I personally email the founder or a director and remind them that we are a small but growing business, and cash flow is tight. I ask them to settle the invoice by the end of the week or let me know if there are any issues.

Seven times out of ten, this personal email will work, as entrepreneurs understand the situation. You may still need to send a final demand letter, and if there is no response, you will have to inform them that you will bring in debt collectors. This is usually enough to prompt them to pay up.

> *Subject: Invoice [invoice number] –*
> *payment overdue*
>
> Dear [Customer's Name],
>
> I hope this email finds you well. I am writing to follow up on invoice [invoice number] that was sent to you on [invoice date]. The invoice total was [invoice total] and the due date was [due date].
>
> I noticed that the payment has not been received yet and I wanted to check if there is any issue or concern that I can assist you with. Please let me know if there are any problems or if you need any further information.
>
> I understand that things can get busy and payments may slip through the cracks. I kindly

ask that you make the payment at your earliest convenience. We appreciate your business and want to ensure that all of our invoices are settled promptly.

Please let me know if you have any questions or concerns.

Best regards,

[Your Name]

Trim the fat

It's essential to keep a close eye on expenses and trim the fat as your business grows. As you acquire more tools, subscriptions and expenses, it's easy to lose track of how many you're paying for and whether you're using them.

I have my office manager keep track of monthly expenses in a Google Sheet. Every three months, I review it and assess if there are any expenses that can be cut. I ask myself if I know what the expense is, if we're making use of it and if it's generating any income. If the answer to any of these questions is no, I cut it. If I find later on that we do need it, we can always review the situation.

Another way to keep expenses in check is to regularly report your business credit and debit cards as lost. All our expenses are charged to my Amex business debit and credit cards. Every six months, I mark them as lost and get new cards with different numbers. This way, I can keep track of companies that have tried to access regular payments from us and stop any unnecessary charges.

Being rigorous about expenses can save you a significant amount of money. In my case, it has saved me anywhere between £3k and £5k a year, which is good news for cash flow.

Reinvesting in the business

The degree to which you reinvest in your business will depend on whether you are in scale mode. Once you get to the desired level, it's all about maintaining profit and taking profit out of the business. One important thing to remember is to pay yourself first.

Let's say you want to take US$250k out of the business every year: make sure you're paying yourself out of the profits first, then covering all your other costs, and what's left over is what you can reinvest. In the case of a recruitment agency, you don't need to reinvest much because it's a service-based industry. If you've got the right systems and tools in place, the only big investment is going to be in staff. As one of my mentors, Felix Dennis, says in *How to Get Rich*, 'Overhead walks on two legs.'[6] If you can build a business without hiring, go for it. Can you do more with less?

In some cases you can. By keeping your staff numbers below thirteen you can avoid the level of support that a larger team requires in terms of HR support, communications, etc. When you're reinvesting in a business, you always need to ask yourself whether it will generate more income. All my employees generate revenue – whether they are a recruitment consultant or a marketing specialist helping to secure inbound candidates. I once hired too many people too quickly (see next chapter) and it cost me a lot of money. Now my motto is: 'Grow slow, hire slow, fire fast.'

In terms of ROI, I would like to think that if I invest US$50k in an employee, they will generate US$250k for the business. I'd say you need at least a threefold ROI, which is what I look for when it comes to marketing in the form of paid ads or organic marketing. With our marketing sourcing system, that return can be as much as nine times. It is a balancing act to maintain ROI as you scale, but if the return should fall below a two-times return, I would discontinue investment

---

6   F Dennis, *How to Get Rich: The distilled wisdom of one of Britain's wealthiest self-made entrepreneurs* (Ebury Digital, 2011)

into that particular form of marketing. It's important to keep track of the ROI of each marketing strategy and make adjustments accordingly to ensure that the business is growing profitably.

From $100k to $1 million

This scale of expansion is possible for every recruitment niche in most locations. Of course, it will be harder to achieve outside of a demand market. The thing to remember is that people are willing to pay more for quick and pain-free recruitment. I've even used agencies to recruit for my own business.

It's for you to decide your ideal level of profit. To my mind the sweet spot is to have a business of around three employees and four remote sources generating between US$500k and US$1m. Many people in my programme have achieved this and are maintaining it successfully.

Your starting point should be identifying how much you want to be earning in three years' time. This will depend on what sort of house you want to buy, what car you want, what sort of holidays you want to take and so on. Think twice before deciding you want to scale up to having a multimillion-dollar business to sell, because, as we know, 80% of businesses don't sell. Even if you're lucky enough to sell – then what? I've got friends who sold their businesses for US$60m and ended up sitting around, bored. Six months later they bought another business and started all over again.

The big mistake is to think that having more employees equals more revenue equals success. So many people that I mentor now have had bigger businesses than mine and made a lot less money. In the meantime, they've become overstretched, working sixty to seventy hours a week with no holidays, and perhaps have a divorce to show for it all. They might have an empire of forty employees, but that means their profits are being spread thinly.

To reiterate: the only thing that measures success is profit. Focus on building a profitable agency with high margins without hiring more staff – in short, a boutique, self-managing recruitment agency that allows you to have a life: to see your family and friends and enjoy your leisure interests. It's worth noting that my agency has ten employees, which is the maximum for a seven-figure recruitment agency before it gets too complex.

Checklist

We have discussed the importance of maintaining positive cash flow in your recruitment agency and highlighted some important strategies for achieving this. Some of the key takeaways include:

- Regularly monitor your business bank account to keep track of liquid funds.

- Calculate average overheads to compare with incoming funds.

- Offer discounts for prompt payment and implement a system for chasing late payment.

- Trim unnecessary expenses to keep the business lean.

- Carefully consider reinvestment in the business to ensure it generates revenue.

- Set lifestyle goals and base growth plans on the income needed to achieve them.

- Check your business bank account at least every week, if not every day, so you know the level of your liquid funds.

- Calculate the average amount of your overheads over three months so that you can compare it with incoming funds over the same period – ideally, your costs will represent no more than 40% of your revenue.

- Ensure prompt payment by offering clients a 5% discount if they settle within seven days and operate an escalating regime of pursuing late payment.

- Keep your business lean by not paying out unnecessarily for subscriptions or other items that are not benefiting your business.

- Decide on the lifestyle you want and base the growth you seek on the amount you need to sustain it.

FIVE
The CEO Plan

My aim is to always have Mondays off. This doesn't necessarily mean that I stay away from the business for the whole day, but I certainly leave the morning clear. There is nothing at all booked into the diary – this is my me-time, for blue-sky thinking. I get a notebook and a pen (no technology, thanks) and go to a coffee shop or some other relaxing environment. Then I just think – about the business and how I can work on it. The conditions are ideal for slipping into a state of flow and releasing my creativity. In the afternoon, I can begin to explore anything that has emerged from the morning and consider how it could enhance my business.

Blue-sky Mondays help inform the CEO plan – the plan that sets out exactly what you expect to do from day to day in your business. This will vary from business to business, depending on your aspirations in terms of things like money, size of enterprise, solopreneurship or team working. The starting point is where you want to end up in three to five years' time, and you work back from that. To achieve financial freedom, you should be looking at bringing US$300k to US$1m of net profit into your business every year.

You're on your own

The advantage of being your own boss also has a disadvantage: you've got no one to tell you what to do, so you're totally reliant on your self-discipline. My great weakness was always getting sidetracked by the exciting new tools popping up in email offers – 'shiny new object syndrome' – and spending far too much time watching the demos and wondering how I could factor them into the business. Before I knew it, two hours had gone by. This is why having a structure to your week to keep you in line is so important. I use a weekly time block schedule to manage my time effectively. I prioritise different categories like self, free time/family, marketing, sales, candidate time, manage, meet and buffer to stay organised and focused on my goals. This approach helps me balance my work and personal life, prioritise my tasks and ultimately achieve success in my business. Everything is mapped out on a Google Sheet: https://docs.google.com/spreadsheets/d/1oVtvQl mdIFwgMJGngkHaNXPO5UvpH-Pf6_Fv2UMJ7ks/ edit#gid=2077496469.

Time management through time blocking

Effective time management is essential to maximise productivity and achieve the desired outcomes. One approach that has been proven effective is time blocking. This technique involves dividing your time into blocks of focused activity to optimise your productivity and achieve a deeper state of concentration on your tasks.

I have personally found that time blocking works best for me in the form of sprints, which are blocks of sixty to ninety minutes. I allocate 100 units of time per week and carefully divide these units between my various activities. For example, I reserve Tuesdays and Thursdays for client meetings, and dedicate several hours in a day for candidate calls. This helps me to avoid jumping from one task to another, which prevents me from getting into a flow state.

According to Mihaly Csikszentmihalyi, author of *Flow: The psychology of happiness*,[7] achieving a deep state of

---

7   M Csikszentmihalyi, *Flow: The psychology of happiness* (Rider, 2002)

concentration on an activity is crucial for both happiness and productivity: 'Flow is the state in which a person is completely absorbed in an activity, and experiences a feeling of energized focus, full involvement, and enjoyment.' In his book, he emphasises the importance of flowing in a task, which can take several hours to achieve. Without this level of immersion, you may only perform at around 75% of your ability, instead of the 100% that your tasks deserve.

Hands off your inbox: make email management a priority

Emails can quickly become a source of stress and distraction, taking up valuable time and energy. That's why it's essential to make email management a priority. One of the key principles I emphasise on my programme is keeping out of your inbox as much as possible.

In the beginning, I found it challenging to stay away from my inbox. I was constantly checking it – opening, closing, replying, saving drafts – and this became an obsessive habit, much like scrolling through social media.

To combat this, I now limit my email check-ins to twice a day – once in the morning and once in the afternoon – and I prioritise my emails to make the most of my time. Client emails are usually urgent and require immediate attention, while other emails can be responded to at the end of the day or within the week. This approach allows me to focus my energy on other tasks and helps me stay productive throughout the day.

It's important to understand that managing an inbox can be a time-consuming and distracting task, especially when checking it frequently and getting bogged down with unimportant or non-urgent emails. By limiting the time you spend on your inbox, you can increase your focus and productivity on other tasks.

One way to manage your inbox more effectively is by hiring a VA who can help you prioritise your emails, responding to urgent messages, filtering out non-important messages and keeping your inbox organised. Here are a few steps to help you get started:

1. **Define your email management strategy:** Decide on a frequency for checking your inbox, such as twice a day, and establish a priority system for handling emails.

2. **Delegate email management to your VA:** Provide your VA with clear instructions on how to manage your inbox, including what type of emails require immediate attention and which ones can be addressed later.

3. **Train your VA on email management:** Your VA should have a good understanding of your email management strategy and your business, so provide them with the necessary training and tools to effectively manage your inbox.

4. **Review and evaluate:** Regularly review the performance of your VA, and make necessary adjustments to your email management strategy.

By using a VA to manage your inbox, you can free up valuable time and energy to focus on more important tasks and achieve a better work-life balance.

Out of your inbox

Labelling	Action	Examples
Urgent	Forwarded to private email for an answer today	Email from candidate accepting counteroffer
Important/ client message	Gets forwarded to private email and Slack message	Client email saying candidate is dropping off interviews
Marketing/ general	Respond once a week	Arranging meetings
Not important	Archive or VA replies	Emails categorised as 'social' or 'promotional'

You'll see from the table that I have a private inbox to which all the most important messages are forwarded. This means that a certain amount of filtering will already have been done, leaving everything that remains in the general inbox to be dealt with by the VA or an office manager – and a great deal more head-space for me as CEO.

A different routine

The job of the recruitment agency owner should be to be the face and brand of their business. My weekly and daily routines are focused on overseeing the business strategy and ensuring that the systems are working correctly, but this leaves plenty of time for pitching to clients.

I flagged up earlier that the business owner should be performing the tasks that generate the highest income, and of these the most important task is speaking to what I call 'platinum' clients. These are the ones you want to engage to work with your agency, who will pay you higher fees and give you repeat business, which you will then hand on to your delivery team so that they can fill the vacancies.

This is my priority, and after that comes overseeing my team. I usually do this through Zoom team huddles at the beginning and end of every day. Slack and Zoom enable me to run my business from wherever I happen to be, and at the moment I have chosen to live in Dubai.

Many people try to sell their businesses after a few years; though, as we've noted, most businesses don't sell. My agency is providing me with the lifestyle I want, without me feeling the need to sell, because I have reached the point where I don't need to do that many client pitches.

CASE STUDY: From burnout to brilliance

Ken was a busy business owner who felt overwhelmed with his workload. Despite having more jobs than he could fill, he found himself unable to delegate tasks and felt trapped on the hamster wheel of daily responsibilities. He was determined to break the cycle and find a way to grow his business.

In the summer of 2021, Ken joined The Agency Blueprint programme and immediately dedicated time to the programme each week. He attended every live call, even the early morning ones, and took action to create extra time for himself. He streamlined his workload by eliminating low-impact activities and improved his cashflow by asking clients for retainers and prioritising those jobs.

The results were impressive. Ken's monthly sales average of US$35k increased to over US$1m by the end of 2022, with a 60% profit margin. He added staff, grew his team from 3.5 to fifteen people in three different countries, and delegated tasks to department leaders. His profits tripled in 2022 and he had more freedom to work on the things he wanted.

Ken credits The Agency Blueprint programme for helping him break the cycle and reach new heights in his business. He is now a coach for the programme and continues to help others on their journey to success. He reflects on his progress with gratitude and is proud of the progress he has made by making time for himself and his business.

Delegating

Delegating can be hard for an entrepreneur at the beginning, because entrepreneurs love control. Don't we all? If you study the approaches of millionaires and billionaires to their business, however, you'll see that they all have the ability to delegate.

It's understandable that you'll find it hard to let go of these things when you've been used to handling the invoices, dealing with the bank, creating the website, communicating with the clients, etc. You can be so entwined in the fabric of the business that you want to oversee every aspect of it – making sure that everything is just perfect. This is one of the biggest mistakes that new entrepreneurs make.

Of course you need to be involved in growing the business, but the business must be its own entity. Developing the mindset of a business owner (as opposed to that of a business operator) means seeing the business as an asset for which you can create a strategy and systems, rather than getting bogged down in the daily grind of everything that's going on. You can always spot the busy bosses who haven't managed to delegate: they're burned out from working long hours every week, trying to do a million and one things.

I learned to let go – to be content with things being 70% done by someone else, rather than me having to do it to 100% all the time. When you hand over the delegable tasks, you can scale more and work on high-income-generating tasks that will help your business to be more successful and earn more money.

It helps to assign a value to your time, and delegate all the tasks that fall below that threshold. When you're starting out, this value might be quite low, so you would only be delegating tasks worth less than US$50 an hour, but it should rise incrementally so that in Year Three it would be up to US$250 an hour, and beyond that it could rise to US$500 or even US$1,000 an hour.

Delegating successfully

The art of hiring successfully is to have the right number of staff to free you from the day-to-day running of your business, but without adding too great a burden of management to your responsibilities. You will only be freed up to work on your business if you're prepared to give them things to do, though.

The benefits of delegating are reduced significantly if you have to spend a lot of time explaining to people what you want them to do. I find the quickest method is to make a Loom video: a screen share that walks the viewer step by step through what I do as I undertake the task live.

Then I get one of my VAs to watch the video and type up a Google Doc, using bullet points for the steps in the process. This is how you build standard operating procedures and it's the cornerstone of systematising your business, because now you have something that you can hand to a member of your team so they can perform the task. The first time you do this, you will need to review how well it has worked and adjust the guidance if necessary, and you also need to be open to feedback from your staff at any stage on the effectiveness of the guidance.

I don't believe in micromanagement and lots of KPIs, and I don't routinely check up on what my staff are doing. If something goes wrong, I will investigate what happened, but as I hire people who are engaged and conscientious, I trust them to get the job done.

I have a minimum number of KPIs relevant to people's roles, because anything beyond this is simply bureaucracy for the sake of it.

The distribution of KPIs according to role

Job title	KPI
Marketing sourcer/ virtual sourcer	• Number of calls booked in for their recruiter per day/week • Number of these that turn into an interview • Number of these that result in a placement
Recruiter/ delivery consultant	• Number of CVs sent per week • Number of interviews arranged • Number of job offers received • Number of placements made

You could add in many more metrics, such as number of conversations held with candidates, number of messages sent, but I don't like getting into that much detail. I would rather just know the key numbers and the direction they're moving us in.

What to delegate

There are many activities in a recruitment agency that can be delegated successfully:

• CRM management

• Monitoring and updating the ATS

• Email campaigns

• Social media

- Website design

- Bookkeeping and finance

I would still advise you to keep overall control of the business finances, though. You need to stay close to the money – it's the heartbeat of the business.

You can probably delegate around two-thirds of the tasks in your business. This leaves you, as the CEO, to be the face and brand of your business and win clients. The amount of time any given task takes up can be surprising: something that takes, on the face of it, only one hour a week could actually consume more like five to ten hours, because you think about it before you do it, you review it after it's done, you think ahead to doing it again next week, and you have to keep reminding yourself to do it – it's all taking up mental bandwidth.

Set this against the fact that you've only got so many units of time at your disposal each week – and not all of these are highly productive – and you'll see how time-consuming even an apparently trivial task can be. You have to ask yourself if that task is worth so many units of your limited time.

Checklist

As CEO of your own agency, you may have to get used to working differently from how you worked before. To avoid getting bogged down in your business, make sure that you are doing only those high-value tasks that need to be done by you, and delegate the rest. The following techniques can help:

- Resist the appeal of shiny new objects in whatever form – they are a distraction from your focus on the core activity.

- Organise your time so that you are aware how much you have at your disposal, and devote enough time to similar activities to get into 'flow'.

- Prioritise your inbox rigorously so that you don't waste time on emails that someone else could respond to.

- Delegate effectively by ensuring that your team have access to all the detailed and up-to-date information they need.

- Keep KPIs to a minimum, but those you do have should reflect outcomes rather than inputs.

SIX

Hiring

Back in 2019, for a number of reasons, I ended up overhiring. My agency had begun to be successful, and we'd moved into bigger offices. In fact, I had taken up an opportunity to buy a commercial office space five minutes from my house. I'd always wanted to get into property, and it made sense to buy these premises.

The idea was to renovate the building and use the downstairs space for the Ronald James headquarters, while subletting the rest of it to other small-business owners to generate extra cash flow. Once I'd kitted out the ground floor, we had space for more staff, and I was keen to take things to the next level. I hired a non-executive director for a brief spell, and then I started thinking, 'OK, why not scale this to between twenty and twenty-five employees? Let's get to US$10m.' (That magic figure that every entrepreneur wants.)

I went on the hunt for some senior people for the business, and we hired recruitment consultants who were already managers in other agencies – three of them came from our biggest competitor. They were all great people, with great track records; they wanted great salaries, too.

I quickly realised that the culture we had created within Ronald James – a positive, close-knit culture based on ten to twelve employees – made it hard for the new entrants to settle in. Despite their wealth of experience, they struggled to adapt themselves to our environment; they didn't enjoy coming from a large organisation into a small one, and as a result some didn't perform as well as we'd expected. This turned out to be a big, expensive mistake because it threatened our culture and upset our team.

The other pitfall of growing too far and too fast in this way is that the added complexity – of systems, of communication – means that things are far more likely to go wrong. As Daniel Priestley says: 'A team of four has six "lines of communication". A team of twelve has sixty-six. A team of fifty has 1,225 lines of communication. The key to exponential growth is overcoming exponential complexity.'[8] You only have to look at the following diagrams to see why this happens.

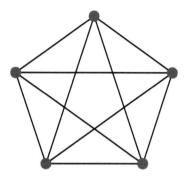

Connections between five people – ten lines

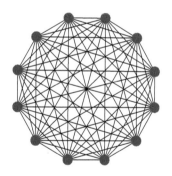

Connections between twelve people – sixty-six lines

8   D Priestley (@DanielPriestley) 'Lines of communication' (6 September 2018), www.twitter.com/danielpriestley/ status/1037752857620037633, accessed 1 March 2023

My mistake was to get carried away with my new premises and start looking for reasons to hire people, rather than looking for reasons not to hire people, which should be your starting point.

After a couple of months I took the decision that the new recruits needed to leave. It was a stressful decision – and an expensive one, because it had cost me a lot of money to hire them, and I had paid them onboarding bonuses. Now I needed to give them a payoff to terminate their employment, but it would have cost me a lot more money and done far more damage if I had kept them on.

The question I should have been asking myself all along was: 'How can I make it easier for my staff to make more money for themselves and for the business, and still enjoy what they're doing?'

How many?

The ideal number of people in a successful boutique business is around twelve. As Priestley advises: 'Never let your business get bigger than thirteen employees. This is the sweet spot to avoid the wilderness stage where businesses are too big to be nimble and too small to have the resources they need.'[9]

---

9   D Priestley, *Entrepreneur Revolution: How to develop your entrepreneurial mindset and start a business that works*, 2nd edition (Capstone, 2018)

If you're going to go past twelve, you ideally need to aim for fifty and become a large company with an HR department and a finance department and training plans, etc. If you look at what most business owners and entrepreneurs want, it's financial freedom and being able to work when and where they want. I don't know of any recruitment agency owners who can take six holidays a year, work four days a week and run a team of thirty-five.

To create a business of ten to twelve people is to hit the sweet spot, where you can be bringing in US$2m a year and your employees are earning good money. The flat hierarchy means they feel almost as if they are running their own mini business within the company. We've got a great office that it's fun to be part of, and we have Zoom meetings every day with our remote recruiters, so they can be part of it too.

Structure

Within the team there are of course people who are more senior than others, and this is reflected in their pay and responsibilities. Having the correct balance of roles and well-defined job specifications is important for the smooth running of an agency. The diagram below shows the structure that has worked well for me over the last five years.

Team structure

The breakdown of roles and responsibilities is as follows:

- **Delivery consultants:** These are the main revenue generators of the business. They are in effect 180-degree recruitment consultants who deal only with candidates. They don't have to worry about winning new business or new clients, though they do manage existing accounts. Once they are fully up to speed, they should be generating between US$30k and US$50k a month.

- **Marketing manager:** This is in effect a sales role, and the member of staff is responsible for gaining exposure for your brand through creating events, running your social media and generating video outreach. (Ideally, I'll hire an ambitious young marketing manager with two years' experience and teach them what I expect from their role in the agency.) They are also responsible for managing the team of marketing sourcers that work with them.

- **Marketing sourcers:** These are the people doing video outreach every day to the candidate market, nurturing candidates, keeping in touch with them and sending them value invitations and possible posts. They are the ones supplying the delivery consultants, so they work closely with them.

- **Office manager:** This role is part facilities manager, part personal assistant in that they look after the physical space of the office, maintain the company culture, organise team events, do monthly round-ups and generally keep everyone happy.

- **CEO:** That's you! You're the one focused on winning new business. You're working on the strategy, pitching, attending entrepreneur events and niche events within your space to gain a profile, creating a presence on LinkedIn and bringing in platinum clients every week.

Just because an agency is small it doesn't mean there is no chance for progression. A marketing sourcer could move into a delivery consultant role. A delivery consultant could become a senior delivery consultant, or you could even bring them in as a director, which would give them a chance to share in the profits of the company.

Your virtual team

Complementing your in-house team is the vital support given by your VAs:

- **General VA:** This assistant does the general admin, including a lot of tasks for you as the CEO, much like a PA.

- **Virtual assistant sourcers:** They do a similar job to the in-house sourcers, but remotely, by fielding a lot of messages and sending out messages to candidates every day via LinkedIn and email.

- **Marketing VA/freelancer:** This role involves doing branding, creating brochures and PDFs, website design and setting up templates. As much of this work is not required regularly, you could outsource it to freelancers rather than assign it to permanent members of your virtual team.

Sourcing your virtual team

There are now several reliable websites offering the services of VAs. I favour the following:

- Fiverr.com
- Upwork.com
- OnlineJobs.ph

My preference is to hire personal assistants from the Philippines: they speak good English and many of them have worked for call centres in the US, perhaps for banks, so they know how to communicate clearly. They are also loyal and conscientious, not least because they may be working to support several other members of their family. We like to have a close relationship with them, and ensure we give them perks that they will value. Above all, we want to make them feel part of the business, so they are part of the team Zoom calls and they are also in our Slack channel. Several of my VAs have been with me for over three years.

Although there are some one-off tasks you can outsource to freelancers, I like to give them to a VA wherever possible. Having different one-off projects – be it recording a Loom video or doing research for you – keeps the work interesting for them, and gives them the opportunity to exercise the full range of their skills or develop them further. It's thanks to VAs that you can have a small business yet act like a giant. The way that one VA can reach out to many candidates is cost effective.

Who to hire

In looking at prospective team members, I'm more interested in experience and personality than I am in qualifications. I ask candidates for roles in my agency to do a Myers-Briggs personality profiling test.[10] It reveals how that person likes to operate: for example, whether they're a creative thinker, an action taker. There's no right or wrong in the results,

---

10   www.16personalities.com

as far as I'm concerned; I just want to know what they're like.

Whatever the personality test may reveal, I also want them to have the quality of vibrancy, which means I want them to come to work fully charged up, energised and self-motivated, because I will not be actively managing or motivating them. Ours is not a Wolf of Wall Street-type business, in that I'm not a motivator. Such businesses are fine if you like that sort of thing, but they rely on the input of large amounts of energy from the top.

To complement vibrancy, I also need candidates to be conscientious: to focus so that they grasp what has to be done, when and how. They shouldn't need telling twice.

Top of the list of what I don't want is egos, because egos tend to create problems. Salespeople tend to have strong egos, but these can unbalance a small company, whereas a larger organisation can absorb them more easily.

In terms of experience, I like delivery consultants to have several years in recruitment and a track record. I prefer not to have to train them up; in fact, I want to benefit from the training they will already have received in their previous posts. I'm happy to train up the marketing sourcers, though.

However much experience people have, I still want them to have that hunger to succeed. You're unlikely to find it in someone who's spent over ten years in recruiting; around four years is the ideal length of time (though having said that, one of my senior delivery consultants has spent around nine years in recruitment, and she still has the hunger that she started out with).

I operate a six-month probation period, though I'll probably know if they're any good within three months. If you're doubtful about them after three months, you'd need to have a compelling reason for keeping them on for the other three.

Though I will train up marketing sourcers in our specific approach, I expect my employees to take charge of their own development. I want them to be learning, so I give them a free Amazon account so that they can order as many books as they want to extend their knowledge and expertise. There are lots of books available to them in the office, too.

We also do a regular 'lunch and learn', when I'll order lunch in for them and run a session on a specific topic. We sometimes have a 'motivation Monday', when we'll have a look at a YouTube motivational video telling the story of how someone has been successful in their field.

Checklist

The ideal scenario for a boutique business is one based on a small co-operative team. This means that you, as the CEO, will have to let go to some degree and rely on your team so that you can get on with working on your business, taking it to new heights. Here's how you build that dream team:

- Identify 60–70% of the work in your agency that can be handed out to your team.

- Provide clear guidance on what you expect and train up where necessary, but don't micromanage.

- Only hire as many people as you need to get the work done; large teams eat into your profits and take up more management time.

- Have a well-defined structure in which everyone understands what is expected of them.

- Delegate tasks to your VAs, who should be made to feel an integral part of your team.

SEVEN
Seven-figure Mindset

I will never forget my first real-life mentor. I'd had lots of virtual mentors whom I'd never met, but I had read their books and followed them on podcasts. Then I paid over £1k to see Peter Sage, a Tony Robbins coach, at an event in London, near Heathrow Airport.

It was worth every penny. He was the one who helped me reshape my mindset and look at life through a different lens. The three-day business-academy-style event was demanding – ten hours a day – but it was full of energy, with people jumping up and applauding, because the messages about fear, belief and mindset were so powerful.

What I learned from Peter went far beyond the law of attraction: he stressed that you are what you project to the world, so it's important to develop a new vision of yourself, letting down your guard and letting the energy flow, so as to create new opportunities in business and in life. You need to support this flow with a healthy mind and a healthy body, so a good diet and meditation are essential. He even goes into quantum theory and how a quantum field connects humans and amplifies success.

I was green at that stage – I'd never paid to attend an event before – and suddenly finding myself surrounded by like-minded people was fantastic. I met someone at this event who has become a long-term friend, and since then we have travelled the world together to learn from different mentors, including the US$50bn man Dan Peña – we went to the brutal eight-day business bootcamp at his castle.

Peter Sage made such a huge impact on me that later on, once I had become successful, I paid around £30k for one-to-one mentoring with him for six months. Looking back, I remember what an astronomical figure that £1k I paid for my first event seemed – but also how it transformed me. Never underestimate the impact that investing in yourself can have.

Developing a seven-figure mindset is a radical move that takes effort and self-discipline. It's a mistake to think that you can get everything you need in this area through Google, YouTube and other online sources. You should start off by finding somebody who's a few steps ahead of you in business and spend time in their company, discovering how they got there and absorbing everything they can teach you.

Find your mentors

Although Peter Sage has been such an influential figure in my life, he is by no means the only mentor I've had. You need a few mentors, to cover different aspects of your business and to provide a balance between real life and virtual, or perhaps local and international. Another of my earliest mentors was a client from the early days of my recruitment agency: we became good friends, played golf and went to see Newcastle United together. He recently sold two businesses for a total of over £60m, so he had plenty of wisdom to impart.

Reaching out

When I first launched my business, I would regularly reach out to other business owners that I thought I could learn from. All I had to do was say, 'You've been so successful. I would love your advice. Could I take you out for a coffee?' I would always bring them a gift, usually a book that I'd come across in my reading that I thought they would find useful.

The business entrepreneurs that I contacted were always generous with their time and gave me some good tips.

Many of these mentors who gave me free advice did so because they could recognise themselves at an earlier stage, some even saying to me, 'James, the reason I'm meeting you is that I see myself five/ten years ago.' They understood the journey I was on and appreciated my desire not only to learn but to relate to them as an individual and engage with them on a wide range of topics from finance to philosophy.

My involvement with local entrepreneurs not only paid dividends in terms of mentorship, but it also established a relationship. At the back of my mind was the idea that we might work together in the future: if they liked me and trusted me, they might one day give me an opportunity to recruit for their company. Sure enough, some of these mentors later became clients.

Looking more widely, you can reach out to potential online mentors via email, through LinkedIn or other internet resources. I've found Grant Cardone and Tai Lopez to be great online mentors, and I've followed their courses as well as others.

In-person network and entrepreneur events have much to offer, but it's important to show up at these events looking like you mean it. You only get one chance to make a first impression, and what you want others to see is someone successful and serious about business. So much depends on how you present yourself.

Widen your horizons

No one mentor can teach you everything, so it's important to have a range of them – experts on whatever it is you need expertise in, be it marketing, branding, sales or personal development. It may be that you will only need mentors in specific areas of business for six months. I would caution against having too many at the same time, though, because you won't be able to take on board all their advice.

Instead of having a few on the go, who might give me conflicting information, I prefer to go all in on one or two and absorb everything I can from them. If I look back at my most influential mentors, I would say that I've got 10% from each of them within me. Of course, I'm not a composite replica of them, because I'm my own person with my own views and values.

It's also important to have mentors that are appropriate for the stage your business is at. As it grows, you will need to upgrade your mentors so that you are always looking for advice and expertise to take you to the next level. It's true that what got you from A to B will not get you from B to C.

To begin with, I focused on mentors who could guide me through the challenge of generating money, as I felt building a solid foundation for my business was the key to everything else. Robert Kohn is a mentor whose work I follow, though I haven't met him. I have found his emphasis on fixing your finances first before moving on to other aspects of your life useful and applied it in my own case. I never got to meet Jim Rohn either, but I have followed a lot of his content because he had such an impact on so many entrepreneurs. (Note that the personal wealth of the mentor is no guide to how effective their contribution will be, though. I've had mentors that are worth US$100m to US$300m, and others who are worth only a tenth of that.)

Input from Peter Sage, Grant Cardone, Tai Lopez and Dan Peña has shaped who I've become, but it has also been tempered with the more spiritual contributions of Sadhguru, and Robin Sharma's blend of spirituality and business – a dimension you shouldn't ignore. General lifestyle advice is more problematic and tends to reflect the experience of those delivering it: the happily married with children will urge you to settle down, whereas those who have been through a divorce will recommend freedom.

I spend the best part of US$200k a year on mentors, courses, programmes and masterminds, because I'm looking for that 1% edge.

Free versus paid mentorship

The input that I got from local entrepreneurs as I was starting out was invaluable, but as you progress, there will be more of a need to pay for mentorship from acknowledged experts. One thing I learned from a mentor is that the more you pay for advice, the more attention you pay to it. At this level, you are far more likely to ignore free advice.

You can bet that when I paid US$30k to attend Dan Peña's castle, I listened and absorbed everything, because I wanted to get my money's worth and a good ROI, which I undoubtedly have over time. Time and accountability are important factors here. You might well be able to pick up all this information for free elsewhere, but it would take you forever to source it and bring it all together. With the prices that Dan Peña charges, you can be sure that he is held to account for the quality of the advice and information he is offering. This is why I regularly increase the cost of our programmes: as our expertise expands, and the calibre of the business owners we attract rises, we get better results – and so do they.

CASE STUDY: Transformation

One client, Wayne from Toronto, recently expressed his satisfaction with the ROI he had got from attending an Agency Blueprint programme. Within a few months he had succeeded in placing fifty candidates with one client.

Weekly group calls

One key element to building and maintaining a seven-figure mindset is the weekly group calls – I call them coaching clinics – that are part of our programme. Accountability, or rather the lack of it, is the number one reason for people not achieving the results they are after, and accountability is what you will find in these calls.

As we know, people tend to sign up to the gym in January, determined to shed the pounds they've put on over Christmas, only to drop out by February, because no one is holding them accountable.

The weekly group calls work because during them you are in the company of people who are in exactly the same position as yourself. If you see those people achieving success, that will motivate you. If they can do it, why not you? You might have to force yourself to show up every week at the beginning – and not only show up but bring something to the table: an action you've taken, an idea you've had. Eventually, though, it will become a weekly habit. Before long, you too will have wins to share.

I'm there to help with strategy. If someone's stuck, I'll get them past whatever's blocking their way and on to the next stage, because it's likely that I will have faced that challenge at some stage. In between calls they can go away and take action and then report back on progress the following week. It's a lot quicker for them to get results than if they had to work it out for themselves.

We cover everything on those calls, from the hard practical financial stuff to mindset. I have to say willingness just to do the work that it takes is often the problem. We're often so addicted to quick fixes that we're reluctant to put in the effort needed, just as people would rather take a pill to lose weight than spend hours on the treadmill.

In business there are no shortcuts. I can give you tools and systems that are proven to work, but you are still going to have to do some work, and the group calls are where your peers call you to account. The group calls also motivate you and give you confidence that you can achieve what others are achieving.

The calls are organised to maximise the value that people can get out of them:

- We do about three calls a week, to be sure that most people will be able to make at least one of them.

- The group size is normally thirty to forty people: big enough to form a community, but small enough to give everyone an opportunity to speak.

- All the calls are recorded so that those who couldn't make it can catch up on what was said.

- The sessions are usually about two hours long, which allows for free-flowing discussion and total immersion in the flow of the session.

If you want to build a seven-figure business, we also offer an elite mastermind, which involves not only two in-person meetings a year at my headquarters in Dubai, but a boardroom-style call with me every week in which we cover the full range of topics and cutting-edge strategies to help you win. You also have full access to all of my team and one-to-one access to me, which will help you plan out the entire new agency model step by step.

The benefit of group calls is that they maintain focus. If you want proof that focus counts, just consider that when Bill Gates and Warren Buffett were asked what they considered to be the number one thing that people needed to be successful, they both answered, independently and without hesitation, 'focus'.[11]

---

11   W Buffett, 'One word that accounted for Bill Gates' and my success: Focus', www.youtube.com/watch?v=ju20hzifwAo, accessed 23 February 2023

Upgrading your peer group

All my mentors stressed the importance of upgrading your peer group. I'm sure you'll be familiar with the famous quote most often attributed to Jim Rohn: 'You are the average of the five people you spend the most time with.'[12] It's a sentiment that mentor Dan Peña endorses.

The truth is that if you are hanging out with people who are off to the pub every night, you will be too and it will distract from what should be your focus. You don't want to be the next bum, so you've just got to do what it takes to get you where you want to go.

I'm still in touch with three people who were in my friendship group back when I started out in Newcastle, and they are all still growing and becoming successful in their own fields. The others, such as former drinking companions, I no longer see, though I know that five years on they're still stuck in the same unfulfilling jobs, overdoing it at the weekends, etc.

The other dimension of attending masterminds in a group of like-minded entrepreneurs is that you are paying not only for what you will learn there,

---

12   C Widener, *Jim Rohn's 8 Best Success Lessons* (Made for Success Publishing, 2014)

but also for the extensive contact with other successful people. No one should be held back by the society or the circumstances in which they are born, and few of us are born with silver spoons in our mouths.

This is also why I joined the most exclusive golf club that I could find. Its members are mostly all millionaires, and while I'm enjoying a round of golf with them I'm also subconsciously reinforcing my mindset. However determined and success-oriented you are, if you're surrounded by people who give off negativity or passivity you will find that you are dragged down. You need people to elevate you, which is why you need to be in the company of people who are at a higher level.

It might not always be about wealth, but I would rather be around ten people who are each worth £100m than ten people who each have only £1k in their bank accounts. Money solves a lot of problems, and it gives you choices. Money can be measured, so it is also proof of being successful. Of course people can live a good and happy life without being millionaires, and most people do, but if you are an entrepreneur and you are striving to be successful, you need to be selective about your peer group.

Networking

Once you've reached a certain level of wealth, you can share ideas with people who are at the same level as you. You can even help one another. You have to come to the table with your own take on things, your own area of expertise, whether it's to do with marketing automation, lifestyle investments like watches and cars, diet or something else. Being surrounded by a good group like this expands your knowledge and your opportunities and is a sure route to advancement.

There are countless opportunities for networking out there, at every stage of your business growth. For a recently launched UK business, I would highly recommend your local chamber of commerce. The mission of the umbrella organisation, the British Chambers of Commerce, is to help businesses connect, succeed and grow.[13]

LinkedIn is another go-to online destination for networking, used by nearly everyone in business, so there's never been a better time to reach out to someone simply by messaging them. You can send a video or introduce yourself in any way you like.

---

13 'Business support' (British Chambers of Commerce, no date), www.britishchambers.org.uk/page/business-support, accessed 23 March 2023

Learning and development

It's worth pointing out that participating in a specialised course will automatically mean that you'll find yourself in the company of individuals who share your interests, and in this way a community – of friends, colleagues, possible business partners and potential clients – is born. For me that niche was digital and technology recruitment.

I could retire tomorrow on the wealth that I have created, but I'm an entrepreneur, so I want to keep going and I'm still learning. I buy a book every day, I read all the time, I attend courses and I study on YouTube for two hours every night – everything from cryptocurrency to investments via philosophy. I'm hungry to keep developing, sharpening my sword and growing my skill set.

If you don't keep growing in this way, your competitors will catch up with you. I picture this investment of time as working in the same way that compound interest on money works. You start off with just one penny, but if you keep reinvesting it every day it adds up to millions of pounds in just a few years' time. The more I keep feeding my brain every day the better equipped I am to maintain that edge. Knowledge is power – but it must be followed up with execution.

There are far cleverer people out there, perhaps working as professors in universities, but they're not as wealthy because they don't put their knowledge to work in the same way. Make sure that if you have the knowledge, you also have a vehicle for using it to scale your business to create wealth, create jobs.

It's important to be patient, though. When it comes to learning, you may not see an instant return on your efforts. In the first three years of my recruitment business, I made good enough money, but nowhere near the amount I am making now. You can picture the growth like one half of a bell curve, with a steep rise following an initial shallow one. By Year Five I had refined my understanding of how my business worked to the point where everything fell into place, and I began to reap that compound interest: finance, marketing, mindset and the rest were all in alignment.

Checklist

Transforming your mindset is essential for a successful business journey, and the transformation needs to be sustained. Here's how you can change your 'lens':

- Don't hesitate to reach out to business owners in your area for advice and information.

- Make the most of networking and entrepreneur events by looking the part when you attend and sharing your knowledge.

- Identify specific areas of expertise in which you need input and seek out mentors who can provide this.

- Don't ignore the spiritual dimension: it helps you maintain a sense of perspective.

- In general, the more you pay for guidance and mentorship, the more attention you will pay to it.

- Participating in weekly group calls is great for motivation, inspiration and being held to account.

- If you want to be a successful business owner, keep the company of other successful business owners.

- True entrepreneurs never stop learning; that's what gives them their edge.

EIGHT
Investing In Yourself

Back in 2015, just before I launched my own business, I was experiencing stress and anxiety. I was working in a large agency, in a high-pressure management sales job, but I was also trying to prepare for going it alone. I was getting up at 5am to go to the gym in my garage in the cold and dark, then listening to an audio book, then journaling. That was two hours of personal development and growth before I even went to the office. I did it because my mindset was already one of 'I want to work for myself now; I want to take my destiny into my own hands.'

It took a mentor to reveal to me what was happening. I'm a Type A personality, characterised by ambition, impatience and a drive to succeed, and I was living on the edge.[14] It was as if I was driving a high-performance car very fast all the time, to the point where it was burning out. I wasn't doing for myself anything like the equivalent of taking the car to the garage to be serviced and for an oil change, and I wasn't putting the right fuel in. I ended up having a panic attack, gasping for breath and wondering what was wrong. It was an alarming experience because I wasn't used to being out of control.

I was so accustomed to going out and about as this suited-and-booted machine, but the machine was running on empty. I was twenty-nine, and I didn't know how to deal with it. Things had to change; I had to slow down a bit.

I was determined to get through this experience without any medication. My mind had got me into this situation, and I would use it to get me out of it. I started looking into meditation and opted for transcendental meditation, which is one of the most popular meditation practices. I began driving for forty-five minutes to attend a small meditation group in the teacher's own home.

---

14   A Sharma, 'What is a type A personality?', WebMD (9 November 2021), www.webmd.com/balance/what-is-a-type-a-personality, accessed 23 March 2023

Looking back, I realise that part of the problem was that I was getting ahead of myself. The people I aspired to be were already worth £100m to £200m, whereas I barely had £3k in the bank. There was such a disparity between my present reality and the future reality that I desired that my mind could not cope. No wonder I was anxious. Add to that trying to cram so much information into my brain, not getting enough sleep and the demands of the day job, and you can see that my problems were predictable.

To make matters worse, I now had all these plans and theories, all these ideas and aspirations for growth that I couldn't put into practice because I was working for somebody else. Of course taking the decision to leave brought its own anxieties, as I would no longer have the security of a regular salary and I was having to pay a lawyer to advise me on the legislation surrounding leaving a company and setting up on your own in the same business.

Round about this time I read Robin Sharma's *The Monk Who Sold His Ferrari* and learned from it that as an entrepreneur you have to feel comfortable with feeling uncomfortable.[15] Sharma is a good writer, and this has remained one of the most influential books in my life. He made me realise it's not all about chasing the money. Michael Singer's books *The Surrender Experiment* and *The Untethered Soul* also resonated

---

15   R Sharma, *The Monk Who Sold His Ferrari* (Harper Thorsons, 2015)

with me.[16] I discovered that if you just let go and let the universe take care of things, as long as you have set your goals correctly and do the right things, you will be OK. What will happen will happen, but you will be able to deal with it.

This period was a turning point for me. I'm grateful for having made that journey, and I'm happy to talk about it because I know I will never return to that point in my life again. Investing in yourself and your wellbeing is not an indulgence; it's a necessity. However resilient you think you are, you need time to recharge mind and body.

Meditation

The brain is a machine – but not one designed to accommodate as much information as we get thrown at us every day, from our technology and from the world around us. The brain is the same machine it was 10,000 years ago and needs to be treated with respect if it is to function at its best.

Starting your day off with a meditation, whether it's for ten minutes or thirty, is an ideal way to build up your brain's resilience. If you can spare that time,

---

16 M Singer, *The Surrender Experiment: My journey into life's perfection* (Yellow Kite, 2021); M Singer, *The Untethered Soul: The journey beyond yourself* (New Harbinger Publications, 2007)

you may well gain about two hours of high-quality productivity in your day. On the other hand, if you launch into your emails and social media the minute you wake up, you'll only be performing to around three-quarters of your capacity for the rest of the day.

I know some people find the thought of meditation – of sitting still and doing nothing for so long – quite challenging. It's often the people who are struggling with this who need it the most. For them I would recommend starting off with a ten-minute guided meditation, which you can get from an app called Insight Timer. All you need to do is to sit somewhere comfortably, put your earphones in, close your eyes and just listen. You will be taken down into a deep state of concentration and stillness, and then you will gradually return to conventional consciousness. Over time, you will get better and better at it.

I meditate for as long as I feel I need to. Sometimes I do a sixteen-minute one, and sometimes one lasting twenty-five minutes. I can now meditate just by going out walking, sitting on the beach or looking at a view.

Binaural beats are also a good way of soothing the brain. These beats are a frequency that you can channel through your headphones to put your brain into an alpha wave pattern, which leads to deep relaxation. You can even use them to help you sleep. You can get these beats through YouTube or as an app.

Daily routines

If you can develop good habits that you practise daily, eventually you'll hardly notice them – but you might miss them when you don't keep them up. If I get off to a bad start by not meditating or writing in my journal or drinking my smoothie, I often find I'm then feeling stressed and eating something rubbish for lunch.

What also helps is to have two or more activities that you do at the same time or as a sequence so that if you're doing one of them, you're also doing, say, the other two; for example, I do the meditation and then drink my green smoothie while I journal, as described above.

To me, these habits now come naturally. Just as with driving a car, where you no longer notice that you're looking in the mirror and indicating, your subconscious takes over. It takes a bit of time to install these habits but once you've put in that sustained effort they will stick, and over time you will see the incremental results. The problem is, most people quit before that. That's why 95% of people aren't successful.

CASE STUDY: Lifestyle changes

Mo is a recruitment agency owner based in London, specialising in building services and engineering. His recruitment business had been running for five years, and his journey with us began at a strange time – mid-pandemic.

Mo's biggest challenge, like many agency owners, was finding the time and freedom to step away from his business so that he could deliver the same quality of service without failing. He was caught in a catch-22 situation, where he couldn't step back from his business regardless of how much revenue was being generated month to month.

If he worked less, he would underdeliver to existing clients. If he continued to be glued to his work, it would be impossible to spend time with his young family.

Mo had to productise his service so that it could stand alone without him and scale up without any stress, anxiety or guilt. As a business owner, his main priority was protecting his time. He believed, 'You can be as wealthy as you want, but if you can't do anything with it, it's worthless.'

To make it clear: Mo's business was doing well, with regular orders and predictable revenue – but he was trapped on a hamster wheel created by incorrect systems that didn't afford him any freedom. As an agency owner, he was also taking on extra responsibilities worth four or five jobs. Mo says, 'It would have only been a matter of time before I burned out!'

His business transformed in just ninety days with us. With the Recruiter Accelerator programme, Mo implemented a proven automation system which enhanced his processes and productivity.

During his time with The Agency Blueprint, we've also seen Mo elevate his mindset by reading books and listening to podcasts, constantly wanting to grow on a personal level. Mo says: 'Because I was reading similar books to you, I might have one day figured out the same systems – but certainly not as fast. I would have made more mistakes, spent more money and we could have been eighteen months behind on the progress we've made today.'

As much of an expert as you may be in your market, in the same way that doctors can't self-diagnose themselves, it is more difficult for entrepreneurs to identify the weak links of their businesses.

Physical fitness

Keeping yourself physically fit is important, but you can overdo it. Working out two or three times a week is fine but four or five, unless you're an elite athlete, is not sustainable. Again, improvement takes time. Strength, stamina and muscle build up little by little. You won't see the change happening, but you'll be able to tell after a few months that it's happened.

The same goes for diet. One Big Mac won't make much of a difference, but a daily diet of them will soon make itself seen and felt. This is why I've opted for a daily diet of green smoothies (among other things, of course). I use a powder called Green Vibrance, which contains trace nutrients, vitamins, minerals, antioxidants and amino acids, along with protein powder – and that's the high-quality fuel that starts my day.

You need to remember that as a knowledge worker, your brain is your tool, and you therefore need to keep it functioning to its maximum potential by giving it the right type of fuel. This means cutting down on sugar and other potentially toxic substances and eating in moderation.

Rest and relaxation

A good eight hours' sleep a night is a sound investment in yourself. I track my sleep and measure the amount of time I spend in deep sleep and the amount of time in REM sleep, which is vital for the creative part of your brain.

Walking in the woods, or connecting with nature in some way, is a wonderful way to clear your head. Walking my dog, Kobe, is one of my favourite daily habits. At one point I used this time to listen to podcasts or a book on Audible, but then I realised it was better to be present and make the most of my environment. My dog was an important part of that ritual, and focusing on the experience of the walk itself helped keep the other rituals in their place.

Reading

I'm an avid reader. I've got piles of books all over the place: on my bedside table, in the kitchen, in the office, in the living room... Although I use a Kindle and Audible, I still take books with me when I'm travelling – sometimes half the weight of my case is made up of books.

What I've found over time, as I've become more successful, is that I've begun to get more selective about what I read. I'm always keen to pick up on bite-sized pieces of useful information and put them into practice.

I should also point out that I don't just read books once and move on to the next one. I often read them three, four or five times, highlighting them and marking them as I go. I return to these books again and again because it helps the information to sink in, and because on the second reading I'll notice things that I didn't see the first time round.

Wealth and happiness

I've reached a point where I can say that the risks I took along the way were worth it. I need never worry about money again. Financial freedom contributes to happiness, which is why Naval Ravikant proposes that sorting out your finances should be your priority, and then you can look to happiness and everything else.[17] Money gives you choices and enables you to buy your time back, or, in Ravikant's words, 'Money doesn't buy happiness – it buys freedom.'[18]

What I would say in this context is, don't put pressure on yourself – you will get there, but you don't need to get there tomorrow. It's a long game, a five- to ten-year journey. Don't make the mistake of linking happiness to your end goal, though, and thinking happiness has to be deferred until you've made your first million. Happiness must be in the present.

Happiness is a choice and, in all but the most extreme situations, you can choose whether to be happy every day. You do this by surrounding yourself with people who generate positive energy, or vibrancy, as I call it. You also need to avoid much of the media, especially social media, and cultivate a glass-half-full approach to life.

Having good goals that you're striving for tends to make you happier as well, as you know that your actions have purpose. I've also learned that starting

17 E Jorgenson, *The Almanack of Naval Ravikant: A guide to wealth and happiness* (Harper Collins India, 2021)

18 N Ravikant (@naval) 'Money doesn't buy happiness' (11 September 2020), www.twitter.com/naval/status/1304349496168 513538?lang=en, accessed 1 March 2023

the day by writing down three things that I'm grateful for naturally increases my happiness.

For an entrepreneur, the trick is to find the ideal balance between striving for more and finding happiness in the present.

Love

Humans, even entrepreneurs, can't get by without love in some form, whether it's love of life, of other humans or even animals. One of the things that transformed my journey as an entrepreneur was when I got my dog, a Maltese poodle called Kobe. His unconditional love brought out my softer side and helped me to be still and calm so I could enjoy our walks and the adventures we have together.

Learning more about the nature of love has also been part of my spiritual growth, so I've studied the works of Osho and of Sadhguru.[19] Robin Sharma has also influenced my thinking.[20] Meditation helps you to experience love as it opens up the heart chakra. It's great if you've got a partner who can share your journey with you, but even if you haven't, love helps you to act from a more positive place.

19 Osho, *Courage: The joy of living dangerously* (St Martin's Press, 2000); Sadhguru, *Emotion and Relationships* (two titles in one volume) (Jaico Publishing House, 2018)

20 R Sharma, *The Monk Who Sold His Ferrari* (Harper Thorsons, 2015)

I feel that love expresses itself in the way that I run my business. I'm kind and fair to my team, but not in a paternalistic way. They have tremendous autonomy and the opportunity to work in a way that suits them.

Whether you call it love or energy or consciousness, keeping this focus as part of your interactions with others is always a positive thing. When I first started out, if I had a problem with a client, I was likely to fire off an angry email to them, but now I've learned to save that email in my drafts, and when I come back the next day, I'll probably delete it, or at the least make it more reasonable.

Checklist

It's easy to put your own needs on the back burner when you're starting and scaling your business, but that isn't sustainable in the long term. Your health, wellbeing and knowledge need investment every bit as much as your company. These are some of my tried-and-tested methods:

- Meditation is a great way to increase your brain's resilience. A morning meditation will leave you calm and focused for the rest of the day.

- Developing good habits allows you to incorporate self-care into your day in a way that feels natural and effortless.

- Getting enough exercise and having a good diet are essential for maintaining both physical and mental fitness.

- Getting enough rest is also important – aim for eight hours of good-quality sleep each night.

- Make the choice to be happy in the present rather than seeing happiness as something to be deferred until you've built up your business.

- Don't underestimate the importance of love in your interactions with others – whether it's with your team, your family or even your dog.

Conclusion

Looking back over the past seven years, I can't believe how much my life has changed. Though my decision to exchange the safety of a salary for the risks of entrepreneurship was scary at times – and I certainly made my fair share of mistakes along the way – it has paid off many times over. The sense of freedom is huge: I'm free to innovate, to develop my own methodologies, to think deeply about my business and where it's going… and I'm free to just go to the beach for the day if I want to.

What's more, not only have I built the business and the lifestyle I aspired to, but through The Agency Blueprint programme, I've had the privilege of sharing my journey and everything I've learned with others, helping over 400 business owners to fulfil their dreams too.

I don't want to do a blow-by-blow recap of the book, but I would like to distil here what I think are the ten most important lessons I've taken from my transition from recruitment agency employee in Newcastle to agency owner and business coach in Dubai.

1. **Decide what you want and reverse-engineer to get it:** The size of your business only matters in relation to what you want out of life, so calculate what level of income you need to fulfil your aspirations, and plan accordingly.

2. **Stay close to the money:** Poor cash flow is a serious threat to any business, so make sure you monitor it closely and correct your course if your position is looking unstable.

3. **Get yourself a mentor, and preferably three or four:** Find a mentor who is a few steps ahead of you in their business and learn as much as you can from them; look out for mentors in specialist areas who can share their expertise with you. I'm delighted now to be mentoring in my turn, through The Agency Blueprint programme.

4. **Build a great team:** Being a solopreneur is fine, but it will only get you so far. Gather the right team around you, establish a great culture and let

them flourish – and make sure one of them is an integrator.

5. **Don't hire too fast:** Only hire when it hurts, so the saying goes, otherwise you will be wasting money and effort.

6. **Don't go too big:** The more complexity there is, the more you will be prone to stress. The sweet spot is a company worth £2m to £3m a year, with a skilled and close-knit team of about twelve.

7. **The more you work on yourself the better:** Whether it's through meditation, diet, exercise or all three, maintaining your energy levels and a clear head will help your business to grow.

8. **Don't worry about what people think of you:** For a while I held back from putting myself out there with Loom videos, etc, wondering what my ex-colleagues would think of me. Most people are too self-obsessed to form any opinions about you.

9. **Be adaptable – things change as you scale:** What served you well at the start of your journey will not do so for the next stage. Darwin spelled out the advantages that adaptability gives you over 150 years ago.[21]

---

21 Charles Darwin's ideas about adaptability and evolution are most famously articulated in his book *On the Origin of Species,* which was first published in 1859.

10. **Choose to be happy:** Don't think you can postpone focusing on happiness until you've made your first million; be happy in the present, whatever your circumstances.

As I look to the future I see even more automation and more AI, and I look forward to leveraging the useful parts of those technologies. There will still be a need for the human element, especially in recruitment, where automation can't replace person-to-person conversations over the phone, on Zoom or face to face.

This is why I'm looking forward to connecting with you. Check out my website, www.theagencyblueprint.com, where you'll see a range of resources on offer. You can access the resources and a link to a free course at www.theagencyblueprint.com/book.

The information on the website should help you to decide which is the most appropriate course of action for you. The Recruiter Accelerator is the programme that will help you progress from billing £10k a month to £20k to £30k. At the next level I've got the Elite Seven-figure Mastermind, which helps you go from £30k per month to £100k per month and beyond.

Now is the time to take the next step and see what the future could hold for you. Contact me via my website or through the social media addresses given at the end of the book, and let's see what we can achieve together.

The Author

James Blackwell is a CEO and successful entrepreneur from the UK. At twenty-one, he started his first business from a coffee shop with nothing but a laptop and a credit card loan. After experiences in sales and a move to recruitment, he found huge success by scaling his market-leading agency to seven figures. Today he runs multiple businesses from his penthouse apartment in Dubai. Through The Agency Blueprint, he helps aspiring entrepreneurs build highly profitable recruitment agencies for the new era.

🌐 https://theagencyblueprint.com

📘 www.facebook.com/entrepreneurjamesblackwell

💼 www.linkedin.com/in/james-blackwell-209162160

🐦 @1jamesblackwell

📷 @theagencyblueprintofficial